International Reserves, Exchange Rates, and Developing-Country Finance

International Reserves, Exchange Rates, and Developing-Country Finance

Edited by
Norman C. Miller
Global Interdependence Center and
University of Pittsburgh

LexingtonBooks
D.C. Heath and Company
Lexington, Massachusetts
Toronto

332.04
I 61

Library of Congress Cataloging in Publication Data

Main entry under title:
  International reserves, exchange rates, and developing-country finance.

  1. International finance—Congresses.
2. International liquidity—Congresses.
3. Foreign exchange problem—Congresses.
4. Underdeveloped areas—Finance—Congresses.
I. Miller, Norman, 1939-
HG205 1982.I55   332'.042   81-47765
ISBN 0-669-04856-9   AACR2

Published simultaneously in Canada

Printed in the United States of America 83. 861

International Standard Book Number: 0-669-04856-9

Library of Congress Catalog Card Number: 81-47765

Contents

Contents

Foreword

When the Global Interdependence Center was first established, as a university-community activity, we looked for specific areas of operation and things to do. Within the economic sphere, we immediately hit upon the idea of studies in international finance, hoping eventually to contribute to the development of a workable world monetary system.

A natural activity in this respect was to hold a world monetary conference. The first such conference, during the fall of 1979, was deemed so successful that a second conference was held one year later, which established a series of annual events. Our thinking at the time was naturally colored by the unstable position of the dollar, the problems being experienced in recycling the petrol deficit, and the wide fluctuations in a whole spectrum of exchange rates. After the breakdown of Bretton Woods-type fixed parities, international economic analysis faced a new challenge, that is, how to interpret and explain exchange-rate fluctuations.

On a transitional basis, the world shifted toward the present system of a managed float after the breakdown of the Bretton Woods system, without having taken up systematically the kind of system that would serve the world community of nations well on a longer-term basis. Options that are presently being discussed are fixed parities (return to Bretton Woods); the managed float, or a freer float; and the gold standard.

The purpose of the annual monetary conference is to take up issues bearing on these choices or, indeed, the specification of a fuller range of choices. The presentations and discussions do not necessarily focus specifically on these issues, but they do focus on problems related to these issues, and it has been the hope of the organizers of the annual conference to produce some action-oriented proposals for a workable system. It may be that some combination of these ideas, or some candidate outside this list, will prove workable.

In order to build up intellectual capital for progress toward a resolution of the issues, we have opened up discussions on exchange rates. How are they determined? How can they be stabilized? How does the system generate inflation? How does the system function under inflation? Indeed, the question may well be asked: What is the explanation of the present inflation and how may it be controlled?

What economic institutions are to be examined in connection with the search for a workable monetary system? This question is central to the final choices. We have a fixed (restricted) parity system functioning in the midst of the managed float, namely, the European Monetary System. Our conference must analyze institutions like these, why they are wanted by member governments, and how they are working. The roles of gold, Special Drawing

Rights, and substitution accounts are examined as specific devices that are currently being used.

Contributing factors to present monetary disorder are the large petrol deficit that needs recycling and the plight of the oil-importing developing countries that have chronic deficits. Many developing countries or poorer countries in the Organization for Economic Cooperation and Development (OECD) group have run into severe problems of debt servicing and overall national solvency. A system and institutions that can cope with these problems are what is wanted. Thus, our meetings encompass contributions from all parts of the world economy. Both the most advanced financial centers of the world and the developing countries were represented.

The issues and questions are now on the table. During future annual conferences we will continue to debate and analyze. At some time, we expect to arrive at a point in the discussion when concrete conclusions can be drawn and some policy suggestions can be made.

Lawrence R. Klein
Professor of Economics
University of Pennsylvania

Acknowledgments

The Second International Monetary Conference could not have been possible without the generous support of the BankAmerica Foundation, IBM Corporation, the Exxon Education Foundation, and the INA Corporation. The Center also gratefully acknowledges the support it received from the Philadelphia banking community. The Federal Reserve Bank of Philadelphia, Fidelity Bank, First Pennsylvania Bank, Girard Bank, Philadelphia National Bank, and Provident National Bank all contributed generously to planning and hosting the conference.

The Center is particularly grateful for the generous and general support given to its International Monetary Program by the Pew Memorial Trust and the Smith-Kline Corporation.

The Center especially acknowledges the guidance the International Monetary Program received from its chairmen: Mr. David Eastburn, president of the Federal Reserve Bank of Philadelphia; Mr. Frederick Heldring, deputy chairman of the Philadelphia National Bank; and Dr. Lawrence R. Klein, Benjamin Franklin Professor of Economics and Finance at the University of Pennsylvania.

Three other individuals and their institutions also deserve special acknowledgment for their tireless efforts to assure the success of the conference: Dr. Corrado Pirzio-Biroli, economic advisor to the European Communities' Delegation to the United States; Mr. Robert Pringle, executive director of the Group of Thirty; and Mr. J.J. Wieckowski, executive vice-president of Girard Bank.

The chapters in this book were originally papers presented at the Second International Monetary Conference held in Philadelphia in November 1980. The conference was sponsored by the Global Interdependence Center in collaboration with the Group of Thirty.

The Global Interdependence Center

Increasing awareness of interdependence in international economic, social, and political affairs led to the founding in 1976 of the Global Interdependence Center in Philadelphia by the World Affairs Council of Philadelphia and the University of Pennsylvania. Now incorporated as a non-profit educational institution, the Center seeks to convene local, national, and international leaders who are personally or professionally concerned with issues in international economic interdependence. The International Monetary Program of the Center consists of the annual conferences, policy-oriented study groups, and research.

Group of Thirty

The Group of Thirty was established in December 1978 in order to explore the basic problems in the functioning of the international economic system. It meets twice a year, for two to three days at a time, to discuss material gathered by study groups and researchers. Some of the reports of these groups and other papers are published.

1

Introduction

Norman C. Miller

The Global Interdependence Center was born in 1976 after the World Affairs Council in Philadelphia held a program called "The Declaration of Interdependence" and a number of conferences in Philadelphia having to do with interdependence. The parents of the Global Interdependence Center were the World Affairs Council and the University of Pennsylvania—what Philadelphians call a town and gown partnership.

The Global Interdependence Center recognizes that in an increasingly interconnected world there are problems as well as opportunities. The Center is not only interested in the substance of problems but in process. How does anything get done in a world with no one in charge? How, for example, does anything get done in an international monetary system that is obviously in disarray? How are the players who can make a difference convened? This point is made by the Minister of Finance of the Philippines, Cesar Virata, in chapter 2 of this book.

Hence, the Center decided to continue to focus on this international monetary area and to organize a second annual conference. The Center also decided that, in addition to a series of annual conferences, a smaller group chaired by Lawrence Klein will, in continuing cooperation with the Group of Thirty and others, focus on substance as well as process.

The chapters in this book deal with two general topics: exchange rates and international reserves; and the financing needs of the developing countries. In all cases, the underlying theme relates to how the international monetary system may be altered to better achieve objectives associated with these two topics. As one would expect, there are healthy differences of opinion concerning how well the current international monetary system has been functioning and what the prospects are for the future if the status quo remains essentially unchanged.

On each issue there are what I arbitrarily call optimistic and pessimistic points of view. The optimistic perspective is that the international monetary system has been doing reasonably well, given the circumstances. Only marginal changes are needed and, even if these are not made, the world will muddle along rather fruitfully. The pessimistic stance is that the international financial world is like a time bomb waiting to explode unless the international monetary system is altered in important ways.

This overview briefly summarizes alternative points of view—including my own—on three major issues. The first deals with inflation and the role

1

played by the international monetary system in creating or allowing inflation to accelerate. The second is the problem of recycling Organization of Petroleum Exporting Countries (OPEC) dollars to the developing countries and the prospect of extreme shortages of funds for the less-developed countries (LDCs). The third and final issue relates to the degree of exchange-rate volatility and to how a Special Drawing Rights (SDR) substitution account might reduce this volatility.

Many economists believe that the old Bretton Woods system was inherently inflationary, because for decades the United States could export unlimited amounts of dollars. Furthermore, some think that the current system may have an even stronger inflationary bias for two reasons. First, we now have several international reserve-currency countries—the United States, Germany, and Japan, for example—that can export inflation to the rest of the world by running payments deficits. Second, the huge appreciation in the nominal value of official gold holdings has not yet, but eventually will be, monetized.

On the other hand, empirical evidence suggests that, during the fixed-exchange regime, the central banks of most advanced countries, excepting Japan, engaged in substantial sterilization activities. Thus, the U.S. payments position may have had a relatively minor impact on the money supplies of the rest of the world. Furthermore, the more rapid rate of inflation since early 1970 might be in part a process of adjustment to an equilibrium in terms of trade between OPEC and non-OPEC countries, which the former refuses to accept. If so, then the inflation rate might accelerate by way of increases in the velocity of money should the domestic and international monetary systems not create sufficient money.

Regarding the second main issue, pessimists talk about an impending disaster in the international banking world, unless the International Monetary Fund (IMF) or other international institutions can significantly increase the flow of low-cost loans to developing countries. Allegedly, many large private banks are very near to their self-imposed limits on loans to several countries. Furthermore, developing countries cannot afford to service much more debt, even if the loans are available. Finally, some economists and bankers foresee a huge shortage of funds available for loan to LDCs unless the international monetary system can be altered in significant ways.

The alternative point of view is that no shortage of funds exists. Indeed, the yields on loans to LDCs have never been high enough to tap the large potential lending ability of second-tier U.S. banks. If a temporary shortage ever arises, then yields will rise sufficiently to clear the market. The true problem is that the market-clearing real cost of funds is going to rise above the almost zero level that has prevailed for many years. This will force a reduced consumption level or lower rate of growth in developing countries.

Thus, we should focus less on how to prevent a shortage of funds—the market will take care of this—and more on how the international monetary system might help minimize the real effects of the likely increasing cost of such funds.

The final issue concerns the degree of exchange-rate variability and how an SDR substitution account might reduce this variability. One argument is that exchange-rate variations can be reduced and LDC financing enhanced by the creation of such an account. An SDR substitution account will reduce the dollar overhang and thereby lessen the potential for destabilizing speculation. The funds in the substitution account can be loaned to developing countries in the form of SDRs. Allegedly, the creation of a substitution account is made even more necessary since Germany's and Japan's payments deficits have forced them to allow their currencies to be held as official reserves. This creates ever-growing magnitudes of reserve currencies that central banks can buy or sell, thus creating more exchange-rate variability.

At present, there are many unanswered questions concerning an SDR substitution account. But before considering these, let me point out that the common wisdom about Germany and Japan appears to be exactly the reverse of the truth. These countries have not acquiesced into becoming reserve-currency countries as a result of payments deficits. Instead, Germany and Japan have had deficits because people want to hold larger magnitudes of their currencies. Exchange rates adjust to make this possible by way of the payments imbalances.

Regarding the substitution account, what will happen to the dollars, deutsche marks, and yen when they are placed in the SDR substitution account? Presumably, they will be loaned to developing countries that will quickly spend them. In a very short time the funds will return to the same central banks that initially placed them in the substitution account. This will have strong inflationary consequences by greatly increasing official holdings of international reserves. Furthermore, unless central bank and other private holders of these SDR assets have preferences that coincide with the composition of the SDR (40 percent dollars, 20 percent yen and deutsche marks) there will be massive buying and selling on foreign-exchange markets as everyone attempts to put their portfolio in balance. The exchange-rate effects of this could be anything but stabilizing.

Cesar Virata divides his chapter into four sections, (1) the supply and distribution of international reserves; (2) the balance-of-payments adjustment process; (3) international saving and investment; and (4) policy implications. The present international monetary system, with its multiple key currencies, allegedly transfers resources in the wrong direction, that is, from developing to developed countries. In addition, the use of simple purchasing-power parity formulas as a guide to devaluations for LDCs is inappropriate. Furthermore, payments adjustment should be oriented toward the supply side of the economy, and the SDR should be expanded in prominence, in part by including gold in the SDR.

In his chapter, Dr. Johannes Witteveen presents an excellent summary of the evolution of the international monetary system and the details of a plan for reforming the IMF and international monetary system by way of an SDR substitution account. One salient feature of the now defunct Bretton Woods system was that it was inherently inflationary because the United States was not forced to curb its payments deficits, and this flooded the world with dollars. Today's multiple-reserve-currency system has a similar inflationary bias, but now *many* key-currency countries can run deficits. In addition, the current system has a potential instability problem, since central banks now have a wide array of currencies to hold and can cause wide swings in exchange rates by adjusting the composition of their reserves. The international monetary system should be altered by the creation of an SDR substitution account that would simultaneously reduce the instability problem and give the IMF ample funds for helping developing countries.

Kurt Richebacher investigates how monetary and financial policies for LDCs may promote capital accumulation and growth. The ability of LDCs to grow depends both on the ability of developed countries to export real capital resources, and on the ability of LDCs to absorb these capital goods. In recent years, there has been too much emphasis on LDC borrowing and recycling in order to finance oil and consumer-goods imports. Borrowing for consumption ultimately leads to disaster. We must focus less on monetary gimmicks and concentrate on ways to decrease government spending and increase capital accumulation in the developing countries.

William B. Eagleson considers the role of U.S. banks in lending to developing countries. He presents many interesting facts; for example, the cumulative claims of private banks on LDCs in 1979 was $150 billion, of which ten U.S. banks had most of the U.S. share of $55 billion. Many of these large U.S. banks have reached their self-imposed risk and exposure limits for loans to many developing countries. Consequently, any future increases in loans to developing countries must come either from smaller U.S. banks—which he believes will not happen—or from non-U.S. banks, official institutions, or OPEC.

Koei Narusawa believes that the commercial banks of the world will continue to lend adequate amounts to developing countries, with very little trouble. However, the LDCs must make painful balance-of-payments adjustments and may need help from the developed countries in the process. This help should include the creation of a new international institution that lends funds for the development of new energy sources in developing countries. In addition, the developed countries must allow the LDC exports to enter their countries more freely. Finally, Mr. Narusawa does not think that OPEC will want to engage in the direct recycling of petrodollars.

Henry Wallich points out, among other things, that international monetary policy is lagging behind domestic monetary policy in its approach. Previously, central banks pursued an interest-rate target in conducting domestic monetary policy, but now many central banks have switched to a monetary aggregate for their target. However, central banks continue to have a target exchange rate in their international monetary policy. Governor Wallich suggests that it may be better for the central banks to decide on a quantity of international reserves and allow the market to determine the exchange rate, especially since the market may know more than the authorities about the level of the equilibrium exchange rate.

Angelo Calmon De Sa presents the Brazilian perspective on LDC financing. Brazil reacted to the first round of oil price increases by borrowing heavily and pushing economic growth. Output grew at an annual rate of about 7 percent for the ensuing five years, but the level of international debt grew rapidly and inflation became terribly high. Brazil has more recently allowed more political freedom, has allowed wages to rise, and has focused less on growth and more on tight monetary and fiscal policies in order to reduce the inflation rate and the rate of growth in external debt.

Roberto Guarnieri shows how Venezuela has helped with the recycling problem in two important ways. First, the Venezuelan Investment Fund (VIF) lends money internationally, for example, a $500 million, fifteen-year loan to the World Bank. The VIF also participates in the Caracas Facility that automatically finances Latin American oil-import bills in excess of some floor. Second, Venezuela and Mexico have agreed to automatically lend an amount equal to 30 percent of their oil exports to Latin American and other LDCs.

Robert Slighton suggests that the main issues in structural adjustments within LDCs are: (1) that domestic prices of oil and other energy sources must rise to equal world levels; (2) LDC exports must rise, primarily by way of exchange-rate depreciations; and (3) capital-intensive techniques of production in LDCs should be eliminated, primarily by reducing government interferences in capital markets that have kept real interest rates negative. Mr. Slighton explains that each of these ideas goes against the grain of the biases of government officials in the developing countries.

Professor Peter Kenen investigates how flexible exchange rates affect both the need and the composition of international reserves. Theoretically, no reserves are needed in a pure float, except that OPEC may want to save in the form of international reserves. Under the Bretton Woods system, changes in international reserves were a result of deficit and surplus countries refusing to adjust. Today, however, variations in reserves are typically a deliberate decision of the central bank or treasury in each country. Furthermore, it is not at all clear that we can now speak of an optimum amount or rate of growth in reserves, and reserves can be created to satisfy demand in a virtually costless fashion. Professor Kenen believes that central banks have essentially completed the process of reserve diversification out of the dollar and into the deutsche mark and other currencies. Finally, he suggests that the international monetary system might move in the direction of limiting changes in the composition of reserves.

Dr. David Lomax's chapter is titled "Central Bank Optimization in the Holding of Foreign Exchange Reserves." He points out that most countries' international reserves amount only to two or three months of imports, and that the volume of financial flows is a large multiple of trade flows. In recent years, there have been two visible trends with respect to reserves, namely that the level of reserves has been growing rapidly, and that central banks are getting far more sophisticated in the management of the composition of reserves. Regarding the latter, most central banks divide their international reserves into several portfolios broken down by currency or time dimensions and let commercial banks manage each part of the portfolio. Dr. Lomax is not convinced that central-bank intervention makes much difference with respect to exchange-rate volatility. However, optimization at the micro level leads to satisfactory results in the aggregate. Finally, he believes that most central banks will not choose the composition of the SDR as their optimal international-reserve portfolio mix, but the SDR may become a very attractive asset anyway.

In his chapter, Dr. William Hood focuses on two main ideas. The first is that a diffusion of economic power has taken place from the United States to several countries such as Germany and Japan. The second is that the concentrations of payments surpluses within the OPEC nations represent a serious problem. As the relative economic strength of the United States declined, the percentage of world international foreign-exchange reserves held in the form of dollars diminished. This has created potentially large foreign-exchange market-instability problems, since now it is possible for central banks to seriously affect exchange rates by altering the composition of their exchange reserves. The large OPEC surpluses are of course accompanied by deficits for oil-importing countries and by the need for massive and costly internal adjustments within these countries. These adjustments will be facilitated by the recent realization by the IMF that supply-side adjustments take time and, hence, IMF loans will be longer term in nature.

Dr. Robert Triffin begins his chapter by pointing out two reasons for dissatisfaction at home and abroad with the present international monetary system. First, inflation has risen to an unacceptably high level, and, second, the distribution of new, nongold international reserves goes predominantly (96 percent) to advanced countries. According to Dr. Triffin, inflation has been and will be fueled by the tremendous increases in base money that have occurred because of a ten-fold expansion in international reserves in the last ten years. Although much of the increase in the value of gold by way of its higher price has not been monetized, it is likely to be eventually, and this concerns Dr. Triffin. With regard to world monetary reform, Dr. Triffin would like to see the creation of more regional monetary arrangements such as the European Monetary System (EMS) and an increased role for the SDR, in order to reduce the dollar overhang and the use of the dollar as an intervention currency.

Dr. Corrado Pirzio-Biroli points out that people have recently put the topic of international reserves and substitution accounts on the back burner, and are now focusing on LDC financing for good reason. The developing countries have been suffering lately. Their real imports fell by 1 to to 1.5 percent from 1973-1979, and their international debts have soared. He does not think that the international system, as it is now set up, can provide adequate funds for developing countries in the future. Dr. Pirzio-Biroli believes that the recycling problem is like a time bomb ticking away.

Dr. Jacques Polak, in his chapter, suggests that twenty countries account for about one-half of the current account deficits of all developing countries, and for 75 percent of all LDC borrowing. The smallest developing countries do not have access to private credit; they need foreign aid and official financing. Dr. Polak believes that OPEC should engage in direct foreign investment in the developing countries. Furthermore, he thinks that commercial banks and private capital markets, in general, must provide the bulk of LDC financing, but these activities must be buttressed by the IMF. We need huge IMF loans to force developing countries to adjust internally to the higher oil prices. This requires much higher IMF quotas, which are now only about 4 percent of world imports, as compared with 1970 when they were 10 percent of world imports. In its lending policy, the fund must continue to include both supply-and-demand management as part of its conditionality.

The position taken by Dr. Alvin Karchere goes against the conventional wisdom that the real price of oil will not rise much during the 1980s. He points out that the forecasts are for a steady increase in demand, but for a relatively fixed yearly supply of oil. Thus, he expects the real price of oil to rise significantly. The average annual rate of increase in oil prices from 1973 through 1979 was 38 percent. Dr. Karchere assumes that oil prices will rise annually by slightly less than half this magnitude, or 18 percent per year over the next several years. This would give oil a price of about $72 per barrel in 1985 and current-account surpluses for OPEC countries of approximately $150 billion in that year. Financing this will be a grave problem, especially for LDCs. Standards of living may have to be reduced drastically unless OPEC foreign aid increases significantly.

Mr. Francis Blee, on the other hand, is an optimist about the future, but he emphasizes that a sudden shock could collapse the entire international monetary system. Such a shock could arise if a key country collapses, if oil supplies from the Middle East are interrupted significantly, or if the real price of oil rises sharply. He recommends that OPEC become a full partner in international monetary negotiations, and that the prices of oil and capital be linked. Most important, he believes that we must induce OPEC to engage in direct foreign investment in the LDCs by having the IMF guarantee OPEC investments from expropriations.

Finally, Dr. Carlos Díaz-Alejandro begins his chapter by pointing out that the first duty of an international capital market is to move capital from rich to poor countries. In recent years, private capital markets have greatly helped Brazil, South Korea, and the Phillippines, but the so-called fourth world did not share in the benefits from the international financial system of the 1970s. Today, most LDCs say that we must reform the international financial markets because the markets do not work well for them. The industrial countries have traditionally said, "No, the system works well," but now even private bankers say that something is wrong, that we need bureaucrats (the IMF) to regulate the international financial markets. Dr. Díaz-Alejandro thinks that perhaps the IMF could prevent excessive competition in international markets and could provide information to all market participants. He concludes by saying that LDC defaults are less likely to arise from increases in oil prices than from recessionary or trade-restricting policies in advanced countries.

Part I
Overview

2 International Reserves, Saving and Investment, and Developing Countries

Cesar Virata

The theme of this book brings to mind the following questions: (1) Is there at present sufficient international liquidity? (2) Is it distributed equitably? (3) Does the present system link investors and savers efficiently?

This chapter is divided into four broad sections. The first deals with the supply and distribution of international liquidity. The second touches on the adjustment process, especially as it applies to the less-developed countries. The third discusses international savings and investment against the background projected in the first two sections. The last section is a recapitulation of the policy implications of my premises.

The Supply and Distribution of International Liquidity

The conventional wisdom is that there is more than enough international liquidity in the world today. This has been said to consist of two major components: the increase in the value of gold reserves and the increase in the accumulation of reserve currencies. I believe that the inflationary increase attributed to the gold factor is somewhat notional. Gold at constant prices, or the physical volume of gold, has not increased as a component of international reserves over the past twenty years. If anything, it has decreased. Gold is not used as an international currency today except as a refuge asset with concomittant effects on gold prices. Gold had become a very attractive asset to hold, and it is used rather sparingly in international transactions and settlement of obligations. Thus gold hardly ever enters into the stream of international liquidity, though indirectly it provides the confidence to gold holders for sustaining deficits. The financing of these deficits increases reserve currencies and adds to the supply of global liquidity. In the process, reserve currencies have grown tenfold in the last decade and nearly eighteen times in the last two decades. In fact, it could be argued that the phenomenon of the gold price is in part simply the obverse of this great increase in the volume of reserve currencies.

It may be argued that the expansion of reserve currencies provided the elasticity in the global monetary system to cope with the drastic increase in oil prices. While the increased financing from reserve currency expansion did assist in the initial adjustment to oil prices, such random and disorderly growth injected too much of a good thing that has now become a major trigger for further escalation in oil prices. In fact, major oil producers have cited the need to compensate for the erosion of financial assets received in payment for their exports.

What is distressing is that this great increase in reserve currencies is cited as the reason why the supply of world liquidity is more than sufficient, and why there is no need to issue SDRs. But this is undercutting international action by national policy; it sanctions the preemption of international cooperation by unilateral action. There may be a sufficiency or even an oversupply of reserve currencies, but there is a shortage of internationally created and managed reserve assets. The SDR, which is supposed to be the centerpiece of the reformed international monetary system, nowadays is quite a sorry record for a centerpiece. The deficiencies in this situation are quite obvious. Reserve currencies are national currencies, and national currencies are issued quite legitimately for national purposes. But these do not necessarily coincide with international needs, so that there is a shortage of the right kind of international liquidity.

The situation is aggravated by the spread of the practice of floating exchange rates for the major currencies. Floating was formerly touted by Western academics as economizing in reserves, since adjustments would be taken out in exchange-rate movements rather than in changes in reserves, but in fact the attention and energy of policymakers has been taken up in trying to maneuver in the shifting currents of rate flotation and in short-term money transfers, rather than in the long-term flows of saving and investment that are essential to the growth of the world economy. One reason for this is that the transactions demand for money as a medium of exchange has been joined and distorted by the demand for money as an asset in itself, independent of its function as a means of payment. To say that there is at present no alternative to floating should not be an excuse for lapsing into complacency; rather, it should be a motive for a reinvigorated search for a better alternative.

A perverse effect of the system is in fact the reverse transfer of resources from the less-developed countries to the developed countries. National currencies used as international media of exchange have conferred the advantage of seigniorage on the developed countries, which can issue domestic liabilities to satisfy foreign claims. Moreover, the deposit in world financial centers in the developed countries of less-developed countries' reserves is an even clearer case of a reverse transfer of resources.

The so-called link between SDR creation and the transfer of resources has been called for by less developed countries in an effort to overcome this perverse effect. It has been opposed on the ground that resource transfer should not be mixed up with international liquidity. But in view of the maldistribution of the proper type of such liquidity, those who oppose the link have the responsibility to come up with something equally good, if not better.

The Adjustment Process

In the international adjustment process, especially as it affects the less-developed countries, the link is all the more relevant in light of the nature of present-day payments imbalances. Formerly, these were most often the result of domestic policies and could be corrected by domestic demand management. Also, under various exchange standards, the objective of equilibrium oftentimes overrode the objective of growth; one could adjust simply by lapsing into stagnation.

Today, this is no longer the case. Growth objectives, both in the less-developed countries and in the developed countries, are internationally agreed to be paramount. Imbalances are not typically the result of domestic policies but are structurally imposed by the workings of the international trading system and the various oligopolistic elements in the supply of capital goods and energy. Protectionism is resurgent among the developed countries, slowing the growth of exports in the less-developed countries.

Many of the international financial institutions that like to preach the gospel of adjustment have themselves not fully adjusted to the new realities. They will prescribe demand adjustments on an individual-country basis. With the severing of the link between currencies and gold, and in the absence of objective monetary standards, they have been basing their analysis and policy prescriptions on somewhat convoluted econometric constructs, such as trade-weighted effective exchange rates, based on the questionable application of economic theories such as the purchasing-power parity theory.

It is not difficult to list the shortcomings of these econometric constructs. Trade-weights, to start with, are not necessarily an accurate reflection of the influence of a currency on another country's trade transactions with a given trade partner when they are conducted in the currency of that partner.

As for the purchasing-power parity theory, Professor Fritz Machlup has waged an admonitory finger at its international practitioners, reminding them that one of its limitations is that it can be applied only after an inflationary period has ended and certainly not during an ongoing inflation. There is, however, little sign as yet that this admonition has made any impression on those to whom it was addressed. Another limitation is that the countries being compared must be in equilibrium in the base period; this bars its use in year-to-year comparisons, especially during times of rapid economic change. A third one is that it is obviously inapplicable in cases where countries start from widely divergent absolute levels of prices. Ignoring this last point leads to perverse effects; the less-developed countries, whose inflation rates may often be higher than those of developed countries precisely because they start from a lower cost-price base, are often urged to devalue, and, in today's world of structural imbalances and resurgent protectionism, can only spiral into even higher inflation rates; they are, in effect, being asked to chase their own tails. Again, some of the international bureaucracies have translated economic theories into mathematical equations as if their being processed by computers imparted to them an aura of Revealed Truth.

The contemporary adjustment process must take account of structural and protectionist elements in an international context. It must therefore be supply oriented and multilaterally shared, and it must have minimum elements for development that are worked out over much longer time periods. Developing countries, therefore, require much greater financing on fairly easy terms, and the burden of adjustment cannot be placed on them alone but must be shared by their principal trading partners.

Moreover, in a world rife with protectionism and structural disequilibria, sole reliance cannot be placed on market instruments such as prices and exchange rates. For the less-developed countries, these may have to be supplemented by quantitative restrictions, unpalatable though these may be to those of us brought up in the spirit of free exchanges. Freedom in this respect, as is many others, is indivisible: if we allow the imposition of protectionist devices by the developed countries, we cannot deny the use of quantitative restrictions by the less-developed countries. I am only hoping that these counterveiling measures will not be applied for they will seriously affect international resource allocation.

International Saving and Investment

Against this background, what can be said about international saving and investment? Traditionally, these have been guided by market forces. In less complicated days, surpluses were absorbed and deficits were worked off by a combination of capital exports and imports, reserve movements, and exchange-rate modifications. At that time, the quotas of the International Monetary Fund (IMF) amounted to about 15 percent of the value of world trade, and it could deploy respectable resources in assisting the adjustment process.

Today, as we have observed earlier, the traditional mechanisms do not work as they used to. Instead of corrective movements, we are likely to get cumulative trends. In the face of structural elements, changes in market parameters like exchange rates and interest rates may succeed in raising inflation and cutting demand without, however, setting in motion the necessary corrective trends to right the situation. The result is slower growth and depressed standards of living.

The unrelenting rise in the costs of capital goods, so vitally needed for economic development, has been overtaken and joined in the decade of the 1970s by increases in energy prices. The developed countries have experienced difficulties in facing the situation, but they at least have been able to offer increased industrial goods, technological expertise, and financial instruments to balance the accounts.

It is the so-called nonoil developing countries that have been caught in the squeeze. Their primary exports are subject to fluctuating prices, their industrial trading partners—facing recessionary conditions—have imposed protectionist measures, and their traditional sources of finance are hard put to keep up the flow of development assistance. The quotas of the IMF have shrunk to a minor percentage, something like 3 percent of the value of world trade, yet the conditionality attached to their use grows ever more severe. Therefore, a large portion of the relatively modest amounts it has to offer remains unutilized.

The first energy shock was absorbed by what has been called recycling, by which the new capital-surplus countries deposited their surpluses in world financial centers that then proceeded to farm them out in loans and investments to capital-deficit countries. But they were funds that could be had only at market rates, and only the so-called middle-income developing countries, with some headstart in industrialization, could avail themselves of this device. Even they have to face competition on the international capital markets from companies with top credit ratings from the developed countries.

As to the low-income developing countries, the situation is one of veritable crisis. Only an increase in development assistance can help them. But the climate for assistance is unfavorable at present.

The observation is sometimes made that the needs of these countries, and in fact of the whole developing world, could be taken care of by intra-third-world transfers. It is said that the capital-surplus third-world countries, which now tend to invest in world financial centers for security and for yield, could divert their placements to their fellow members in the third world. But even with their placements in the developed countries, the capital-surplus developing countries are increasingly reluctant to exchange appreciating natural assets for depreciating financial assets.

Future Action

Since individual capital markets cannot provide the desired stability, the answer seems to lie in international action. What follows is a recapitulation of the steps I believe should be taken, some of which have been implicit or explicit in the earlier sections of this chapter.

What is called for is nothing less than the resumption of the effort at international monetary reform, which came to a temporary halt with the Jamaica agreement of 1976 and the adoption of the Second Amendment to the Articles of Agreement of the IMF.

In this resumed effort we must aim at substantially reducing the reserve role of national currencies, whose disadvantages and perverse effects I have referred to earlier, and seek to establish more objective monetary standards, both in the conduct of international payments and in their analysis.

Insofar as analysis is concerned, this requires doing away with any reliance on synthetic statistical substitutes based on the purchasing-power parity theory for purposes of policy recommendation in the field of foreign exchange, especially for short-term year-to-year changes, as they are more likely than not to lead to higher inflation and slower growth.

Regarding conduct, what is needed is the promotion of an internationally created and managed reserve asset with stable purchasing power, greater utility, and less dependence on the vagaries of national policies. This is of course the SDR, but with improved features such as, among others, unquestionable liquidity not dependent on a designation process, usability in open-market operations and foreign-exchange market intervention, and private ownership. The reintroduction of a gold element in its valuation is a feature that I believe would make it a more objective monetary standard and give it greater market acceptance.

In promoting the SDR the link to resource transfer sought by the developing countries must be given its proper place, if only to offset the maldistribution of international liquidity and the perverse effects, such as the reverse resource transfer, inherent in a system that is now dependent on national currencies as international reserve assets.

In moving toward asset settlement and making an improved SDR the genuine centerpiece of a reformed international monetary system, thought must be given to an intermediate procedure to work off the so-called overhang of national currencies used as reserve assets. This would be a substitution account that would avoid the features that led to the shelving of the last proposal and that would give more heed to the concerns of the less-developed countries.

It is not enough, however, simply to devise new international reserve assets. There has to be a new approach to the international adjustment process. It must be recognized that present-day imbalances, unlike those of two or three decades ago, are more often than not structural in origin and cannot be separated from growth objectives. This means that the adjustment process must work itself out over longer time periods, require more financing on relatively easy terms, and be supply oriented and multilaterally shared.

One manner of multilateral sharing is to reduce and eliminate protectionism by developed countries against the exports of the less-developed countries; one way of providing more financing for longer periods on easy terms is to establish a facility similar to the oil facility of former years.

To assist the adjustment process, the IMF must be given adequate resources akin to equity capital. This means a substantial increase in quotas, to the point where their level is restored to the ratio they bore to world trade before the explosive growth of reserve currencies that commenced in the late 1960s. These quotas, however, must be more reflective of present-day realities and require not only a recomputation of existing quotas based on existing formulas, but perhaps even the devising of a new formula.

Finally, the international community must recognize that there are many developing countries—the so-called least-developed countries—that cannot secure financing at market rates but must depend on concessional resource transfers. For those countries, level of Official Development Assistance must increase in both absolute and relative terms.

All this will not be easy, and it will take all the energy, the intelligence, and goodwill of the participants. But it must be done if we are to match international savings and investment in the great struggle to lift mankind up to higher levels of living.

Discussion

Question: I do not understand the connection between the existence of reserve currencies and what you call the reserve-transfer process. Could you please explain this a little?

Answer: What I was trying to convey is that it is currently the practice of the developing countries to deposit their holdings of reserve currencies in the financial institutions of the developed countries. Thus, there is this reverse flow of reserves, and it has a perverse effect on the flow of real goods and services.

Question: You referred to the SDR in a number of your comments. Do you foresee the use of the SDR by major OPEC or oil-producing countries as a means of settlement for their oil?

Answer: I really do not know, but this may happen, especially since some of the OPEC countries have already created their own basket of currencies that is similar to the composition of the new SDR as of 1 January 1981. I am hopeful that the SDR will someday be used as a means of settlement.

Question: Would it really make any difference to the reserve-currency countries if reserves are placed directly with them, or if you put your reserves in SDRs in the IMF, and then have the IMF place the funds in interest-earning dollar, sterling, and deutsche mark assets?

Answer: Since the SDR represents a basket of currencies, its value moves with the average of the individual currencies. There will always be good and bad performers within the basket. If you happen to always select the good ones you will win over the SDR. There is no way to avoid this.

Question: Would you argue that the reserve-currency countries receive seigniorage if assets denominated in the reserve currency offered a positive real rate of return?

Answer: Yes. What I envision is that we someday have a world wherein all deficit countries should be required to borrow from the IMF, and not be able to issue currencies. Currently, all developing and most developed countries have to borrow from the Fund to finance their payments deficits, but the few key-currency countries have the privilege of just printing money to cover their deficits. I think that we need to establish a world order in which all countries are subject to the same rules.

Question: It is generally perceived that the world economy is oozing with liquidity, Mr. Minister, and then in your remarks you imply that we have some kind of shortage, and that we need to have more SDRs to pump up world liquidity. Could you somehow reconcile these two points of view for us?

Answer: The problem with the issuance of the SDR is that it has taken the marginal or residual role. Everyone argues that there is too much liquidity, and that we should not issue SDRs, but key-currency countries continue to create more money that ends up, in part, as international reserves. What I am saying is that we should stop the practice of issuing national currencies, and should depend more on an internationally created asset such as the SDR. If somebody needs liquidity, they should borrow from the Fund.

3 Managing Reserves in the 1980s

H. Johannes Witteveen

Evolution of the Monetary System

To gain a clear focus on international reserve problems in the 1980s it seems useful first to go back and see how the present situation has evolved over time. We must begin then with a look at the *orthodox gold standard*.

As long as central banks followed the rules of the game of this system, it was internationally balanced. Balance-of-payments disequilibria brought about gold movements, and these in turn induced a decrease in the money supply in the deficit country and an increase in the surplus country. In this way, symmetrical adjustment processes were set in motion in both countries. A new equilibrium of the balance of payments was the result. In the process a balance between inflationary and deflationary forces in the international economy as a whole was maintained.

Gradually deviations from this system in its pure form developed. On the one hand governments and central banks became more reluctant to observe the rules of the game. A tendency to *manage* the system developed. This was, however, more difficult for deficit countries than for surplus countries. For as long as governments wished to keep to the gold standard, gold losses sooner or later had to be stopped by deflationary policies. In this respect the system developed a deflationary bias. This asymmetry remains true today; deficit countries are always under greater pressure to adjust than surplus countries.

Another tendency developed, however, when the gold standard evolved into a *gold-exchange standard*. When central banks began to invest part of their reserves in short-term investments in an important gold-convertible currency, a very different element of imbalance was introduced. This evolution was of course the beginning of a reserve-currency role for the pound sterling. This new element had inflationary consequences in two respects: (1) The transition from a gold standard into a gold-exchange standard meant a capital inflow into the reserve-currency country with inflationary consequences for the money supply. This brought about an inflationary bias because no compensating capital exports and reductions of the money supply took place in the country that started to invest its gold reserves in a reserve currency country. (2) There is a consequence after the transition process; when a sufficient number of countries has substituted reserve-currency claims for an important part of their gold reserves, so that balance-of-payments disequilibria are mainly met by changes in reserve-currency holdings, this has important consequences for the reserve-currency country. A balance-of-payments deficit for the reserve-currency country will then be more or less automatically financed by increased holdings of its currency by central banks in surplus countries. In this way the international monetary situation will be tilted in the direction of inflation as soon as the reserve-currency country develops a deficit on its balance of payments. It has to be clearly understood that this automatic financing by central banks in surplus situations is separate from any private capital movements that may be part of the equilibrium mechanism of the balance of payments.

The disadvantage and ultimate danger of this system is that the automatic financing of reserve-country deficits will weaken the equilibrium process of the balance of payments. In this way a fundamental disequilibrium may develop that will gradually weaken the reserve currency because gold reserves diminish while short-term liabilities increase. In this way confidence, which is essential to the system, is undermined.

This process finally brought about the abandonment of the gold-exchange standard. In 1971 the U.S. administration concluded that it was no longer reasonably possible to maintain the convertibility of the dollar into gold at a fixed price. With that decision the system changed into a *dollar standard*. As central banks, nevertheless, continued to accept the dollar as reserve currency, the situation where U.S. balance-of-payments deficits were financed automatically by central banks in surplus countries also continued. This created the well-known inflationary imbalance in the system that led to growing resistance by European surplus countries.

This development gained even larger dimensions by the rapid development of the Eurodollar market (and the later, more generally off-shore dollar markets). With the development of this market central banks began to invest their surpluses partly in this market instead of in the United States. Through the intermediary of these markets the surpluses were made available for *all creditworthy deficit countries*. All these countries could, by borrowing in the Euromarket, in fact finance their deficits out of the increases in reserves of surplus countries. In this way the inflationary bias of the dollar standard was generalized, bringing about a rapid and uncontrolled growth in international liquidity.

Finally, however, this evolution began to run into difficulties. The accelerating increase in dollar reserves, as well as in private dollar holdings in the Euromarket, became a separate element of pressure on the dollar exchange rate. It became apparent that there was an oversupply of dollars in reserves and in capital markets. The chronic weakness of the dollar, which was a consequence of this situation, further undermined the willingness in the system to continue to hold the increasing amounts of dollar liquidity.

The Present Monetary Situation

This brings us to the present stage of monetary evolution, which can be characterized by a growing tendency of central banks to reserve diversification. Both the weakness of the dollar and a general approach to portfolio management by central banks showed the desirability of partially replacing dollar reserves by holdings of other important currencies that were considered as strong: the German mark, the Japanese yen, and the Swiss franc. This leads us into a *multiple-reserve-currency system*.

What are the implications of this system that is now developing? It seems clear that not one but several reserve-currency countries will now gain a potential to finance balance-of-payments deficits more easily. This possibility happens to fit very well in the present international situation, where Germany and Japan have developed balance-of-payments deficits because of oil price increases. These deficits have to be financed for the time being. It is therefore helpful that a substantial part of the oil deficit occurs in these countries and can therefore be financed by growing holdings of their currencies in reserves.

Nevertheless, apart from the present rather abnormal situation, this development into a multiple-reserve-currency system gives cause for concern. We could say that if the three largest industrial economies all have a reserve currency, and therefore would be able to finance deficits easily, the international system would always be more exposed to inflationary tendencies. For a deficit in any of these countries could lead to inflationary financing out of central-bank reserves. The situation for one of several reserve-currency countries is different, however, from that of one very dominant reserve country, as the United States has been during the period of the dollar standard.

In the multiple-reserve-currency standard central banks in surplus countries have a choice with respect to the currency they wish to accumulate. This was not the case in the pure dollar standard, where the only choice was either to let the exchange rate move up or to accumulate dollars. This possibility for reserve-holding central banks, to choose what currency to accumulate or even to shift its holdings from one currency to another, creates an additional instability in the monetary system.

These changes in the composition of reserves will influence exchange markets. As central banks will generally be inclined to move to currencies that are considered strong and attractive and whose exchange rates are therefore moving upward, their actions could easily strengthen tendencies, which are already present in exchange markets, to excessive movements, overshooting, and so on.

Because of this risk the authorities in reserve countries will have to be very careful to maintain international confidence in their currencies. This will strengthen the dependence of their policies on external considerations and expectations. In certain cases—and this seems to be the case in Germany at present—this can make it more difficult for governments to follow monetary policies that would be appropriate from an internal point of view. But even with some priority for external considerations, the monetary situation in a reserve-currency country can become subject to strong additional external pressures by large inflows or outflows of central-banks reserves. In the present situation this seems to place a heavy extra burden on the United Kingdom. The pound sterling has recently again been considered as an attractive currency, so that the pound is beginning to regain a reserve-currency role, notwithstanding the international agreement of a few years ago to reduce and gradually abolish the reserve role for this currency. Large investments by surplus—mainly OPEC—countries in the United Kingdom have pushed up the exchange rate of the pound to a larger extent than would otherwise have been a natural consequence of North Sea oil and of the strict monetary policies of the British government. This, of course, could have grave consequences for British industry.

The question then arises how this evolving multiple-reserve-currency system could be managed in such a way that serious dangers just enumerated can be contained or eliminated. We already see a tendency at the moment of monetary authorities in the new reserve countries to begin to offer special central-bank paper to surplus countries. The objective is to channel some of the additional holdings of their currencies from offshore markets to the central bank. At the same time certain restrictions on capital imports are being lessened or eliminated, which will also channel some of these investments from offshore markets into internal markets. The intention is in this way to gain a somewhat greater influence on the investment of these reserves and to limit their inflationary potential.

In this context the German monetary authorities have begun to cooperate with some OPEC countries and especially with Saudi Arabia. The question then arises what would be the most appropriate form for such investments of reserves in a new reserve currency. To make the system somewhat more stable, medium-term paper would seem advisable; but then investors will certainly wish this paper to be marketable. This of course would still keep the possibility open for shifts in reserve holdings that could disturb exchange markets. The only element that could perhaps be considered to make these risks more manageable would be a requirement for advance notice for withdrawals of these reserve holdings.

In the report of the Group of Thirty on "Reserve Assets and a Substitution Account: Towards a Less Unstable International Monetary System" some consideration was given to possible ways in which the official international community might handle moves to reserve diversification in such a way that any disturbance as a consequence of it would be minimized. The suggestion was made that "potential reserve diversifiers might give formal or informal undertakings only to diversify their reserves in line with prearranged guidelines—such as an agreement on their part to acquire no further holdings in Eurocurrencies—in return for a degree of access to the money and capital markets of the new reserve centres."[1]

This would go much further than the kind of bilateral arrangements that have now resulted from the cooperation of the German and Saudi monetary authorities. A very large number of countries should be involved in this attempt; and some agreement should be reached about the extent, the direction, and the speed of diversification that is desired, on the one hand, and that would be accommodated on the other hand by new reserve-currency countries. And it would be even more important that this diversification would be maintained in a stable manner after having been brought about. It seems clear that all this will be extremely difficult and perhaps impossible to achieve. For that reason it might be worthwhile to think of the possibility of developing some general guidelines for reserve policies in the IMF.

The amended IMF Articles of Agreement offer some basis for such an attempt in Article VIII, point 7, indicating that "each member undertakes to collaborate with the fund and with other members in order to ensure that the policies of the member with respect to reserve assets shall be consistent with the objectives of promoting better international surveillance of international liquidity and making the special drawing right the principle reserve asset in the international monetary system."

It is interesting to note in this context that even before the second amendment of the Articles in 1974 in the context of the guidelines for floating, the IMF Executive Board had agreed on guidelines for floating, which included a very general indication with respect to intervention. These guidelines, which were the result of clear thinking by the late Marcus Fleming and carefully balanced discussions in the Executive Board still represent a worthwhile effort at international cooperation. The main idea of the guidelines for floating was the desirability of "leaning against the wind," which in fact, in recent years of floating, has been widely practiced. The guidelines added the possibility for more aggressive intervention, if this would be necessary to move the exchange rate into a "target zone" that would have been agreed with the IMF, an idea that has not been put into practice.

In this context the sixth guideline suggests that "mutually satisfactory arrangements might usefully be agreed between the issuers and users of intervention currencies, with respect to the use of such currencies in intervention. Any such arrangements should be compatible with the purposes of the foregoing guidelines."

This would imply that central banks in choosing their currency for intervention—or in changing the composition of their reserves—should buy a falling currency or sell a rising one, thus strengthening the policy of "leaning against the wind." At least one could say that these guidelines would mean that they should not do the opposite—which is of course exactly the risk in the multiple-currency-reserve system.

An agreement along the lines of these 1974 guidelines would indeed seem to be extremely useful. One could even add certain rules about the way in which a desired diversification of reserves could be achieved. In line with these guidelines (see guideline 4) central banks should then buy more of a newly desired reserve currency in periods when it would be weak, and they should sell less of it during a time when it would be strong.

An attempt to reach agreement about such general guidelines will certainly also be quite difficult. Nevertheless, it could and should be attempted. Any progress in this direction will help. It could at a minimum make central banks more conscious of the wider consequences of their reserve policies for the stability of the system as a whole. The chances seem small, however, that such an attempt at international cooperation will go far enough to contain the potential instability in the system.

Moreover an important disadvantage of the system will remain that balance-of-payments disequilibria between the major industrial countries would generally tend to be handled with an inflationary bias. This tendency would even be stronger as progress would be made in the direction of the guidelines that were suggested. For if all central banks in their reserve policies would "lean against the wind," this would in fact facilitiate balance-of-payments financing for any reserve country.

For these reasons a complement or an alternative to these attempts to cooperative management of a multiple-reserve system must remain the *creation of a substitution account*. The scheme for such an account, which had been prepared by the Executive Board of the Fund, did not meet with agreement in the Interim Committee in Hamburg in April, 1980. Nevertheless the Executive Board has been asked to continue studying the subject. Meanwhile the board has decided to simplify the composition of the SDR basket, which will now comprise only the five major currencies.

In its report on "Reserve Assets and a Substitution Account," the Group of Thirty made some suggestions that would make the new SDR claims to be created by the account more attractive. The main suggestion was to bring about the desirable liquidity of the claims, not so much by complicated Fund regulations about designation and acceptance, but by making these claims marketable. The idea was to develop a private market in these SDR claims, so that central banks could sell them in this market at any time. This would also open the way for interventions in special drawing rights. In order to ensure that the market price would remain close to par, the claim would have a floating interest rate that would be adjusted over regular intervals by reference to the average of Eurocurrency rates of the major currencies. This would be done on the basis of such a formula that no significant deviations from par would result. The hope was expressed that central banks might strengthen the official character of the claims through the requirements they place on their commercial banks.

Such a substitution account would bring major advantages to the international monetary system, including: (1) the desire to diversify reserves would be met without market disturbance; (2) it would create a larger, stable element in international reserves; (3) the way would be opened for the intervention in special drawing rights; this could lead to a situation where special drawing rights would be considered as the internationally respectable reserve asset, so that it would become customary to cover deficits at least partially by SDRs. This would begin to counter the inflationary bias of the monetary system.

The difficulty in creating a substitution account—which was mainly responsible for the failure of the negotiations—lies in the exchange-rate and interest-rate risk, which results from a situation where SDR-denominated claims would be given out, whereas against this the account would invest in dollar claims. The necessity to have guarantees to cover these risks was a stumbling block in the negotiations; this was also one of the elements that made the account look rather unattractive to developing countries.

Giving some fresh thought to the idea of the substitution account, the question could indeed be asked whether it would be reasonable and internationally balanced that the substitution account would invest all its funds in the United States. This would be all right if all the money would come out of existing reserves that were held in the United States.

But very often dollar reserves are held in offshore markets; participation in the substitution account would then lead to withdrawals from these markets, which would have a tightening effect. This would make balance-of-payments financing even more difficult for nonoil developing countries. In this context the report of the Group of Thirty recommended that a substitution account should also have the option to invest in these offshore markets.

However, substitution funds may also come from current surpluses, especially from OPEC surpluses. The overriding need, then, is for adequate recycling mechanisms, which would provide financing for deficit countries. As a larger role in recycling for the IMF is now clearly recognized—and as the IMF needs more funds for this purpose—it would seem illogical to channel the substitution funds back into the markets. Direct lending by the account to deficit countries, under adequate Fund conditionality, seems an ideal solution, which would combine a solution to present needs with a long-term improvement in the monetary system.

This source of funds would make it possible for the IMF to extend longer-term loans—this is exactly in line with present needs—where difficult and time-consuming structural adjustment problems in the energy field play an important role. These loans to deficit countries could be denominated in special drawing rights, eliminating the exchange-rate and rate-of-interest risk.

That part of the substitution funds that would originate in existing reserves should be available to compensate for reductions in holdings of reserve currencies, either in the respective reserve countries or in offshore markets. There seems to be no clear reason why investments in reserve countries could not also be denominated in special drawing rights. And as a private market in SDR claims would develop, it would also be possible for the account to place funds, insofar as needed, in offshore markets in SDR-denominated forms. In that case the exchange-rate and rate-of-interest risk could be completely eliminated, and the financial problem of maintaining balance in the account and the need to have guarantees against possible losses on this score would disappear. An important stumbling block in the negotiations would thus be taken away.

It would be possible to develop along these lines a simpler *substitution-recycling mechanism*. Such a scheme would have decisive advantages:

1. It would create an adequate long-term recycling mechanism that could give crucial help, especially to many nonoil developing countries. In fact, it would show a certain resemblance to the idea of the "link," although it would be unobjectionable from a monetary point of view: it would channel growing world reserves to developing countries in deficit, but without adding to total international liquidity;
2. It would offer OPEC a diversified reserve asset, closely comparable to bank deposits in its conditions, and without risk of one-sided political measures by an individual reserve country;
3. It would perform this function without further maturity transformation from short-term deposits into medium- and long-term loans. In fact, it would involve an inverse maturity transformation: from permanent SDR claims to medium- or longer-term loans. This would provide a healthy balancing element in the financial system, where the very extensive growth of maturity transformation by the banking system is beginning to cause serious concern;
4. It would, as in the earlier substitution-account proposals, guide the diversification tendency away from a multi-currency into a more SDR-oriented system, creating a more stable element in international reserves.

I hope that in the coming year—with elections in the three major industrial countries, the United States, Japan, and Germany behind us—the international community will be able to initiate a creative and innovative approach to our monetary problems. As I put it in the introduction to the annual report of the Group of Thirty:

The present serious challenges to the international economy could gradually begin to open the way for a new and somewhat more fundamental discussion on international monetary reform and co-operation. It is important to set this discussion on a fruitful course. The world is certainly in great need of innovative forms of international co-operation.

Notes

1. See H. Johannes Witteveen et al. *Reserve Assets and a Substitution Account: Towards a Less Unstable International Monetary System* (New York: Group of Thirty, 1980), p. 17.

2. H. Johannes Wittereen, *Annual Report, 1980* (New York: Group of Thirty, 1980), p. 6.

Discussion

Question: Your program for the solution of the international monetary dilemma is very encouraging. To what extent does the success of this program depend upon a reduction in the rate of inflation in the Western democracies and especially in the United States?

Answer: I do not think it depends on it. However, I would hope that the inflationary pressures would be reduced as we move in the direction of my program. Our international monetary system influences the strong inflationary pressures that exist in most economies, and it seems to me that if we move in the direction I have suggested, we could come to a more balanced system with less inflation.

Question: A multi-currency system that allows for some central-bank portfolio diversification might have greater flexibility than an SDR scheme wherein the relative weights of each currency are fixed. Would you comment on that, please?

Answer: Certainly it is true that a multiple-currency system gives more flexibility to central banks, but it creates additional instability in the system when banks move from one currency to another. I think we have to keep in mind that the primary task of central banks should be to work for stability in the system, and not to make profits. Therefore, I think that the fixed-basket SDR system is better because it provides more stability.

Question: Where does your proposal stand as far as negotiations are concerned? Is it being considered? Is it likely to make progress?

Answer: As I mentioned, during the recent annual meeting of the Interim Committee, it was agreed that the Board of the International Monetary Fund should again study the substitution account. I think this will be done in the course of the year but, of course, nobody knows how it will go.

Question: When you use the term "substitution account," are you not really talking about a different animal than the usual meaning, in the sense that you are concentrating on the recycling issue. The original substitution account that was considered by the IMF did not have to do this and, hence, is it not the original substitution account that you are talking about?

Answer: Yes, it is a new approach. The substitution account wherein central banks acquire SDRs instead of dollars is the same, but there is a difference in the way in which the account would invest the proceeds. To the extent to which it is desirable, part of the proceeds could be used to finance deficit countries. In any system, however, the surpluses have to be recycled and rechanneled to deficit countries in some way.

Question: Under your proposal, does the IMF do the lending to the developing countries, and, if so, are you going to weaken the "principle of conditionality" of the IMF under your proposal?

Answer: I said this would be done under the normal Fund conditionality. Adequate conditionality would be the important thing.

Question: Have you any comments on the possibility of the IMF taking funds from the commercial markets, which was a topic discussed at this meeting last year? This seems like a simple negotiation in the IMF context. Funds would be taken in SDRs from the commercial banks and then lent on.

Answer: This is also a good idea. I have been in favor of it for some time, especially because of certain political difficulties in borrowing from surplus countries.

Question: The ideas of a substitution account and the recycling question have entirely different time dimensions. We just failed on the idea of a substitution account, and it now looks as if any success on that subject is years away. However, recycling is acknowledged by everyone to be urgent. Is there not a risk in the idea of combining a recycling proposal with an SDR substitution account?

Answer: I certainly do not think that any study of this plan, which will take time, should stand in the way of the urgent need for the Fund to borrow more money for the present immediate recycling needs.

Question: How much of a magnitude do you have in mind for the substitution account? Are you talking about a few billion dollars or $50 billion? Or $100 billion?

Answer: When the plan for a substitution account was originally discussed, the idea involved about SDR 50 billion, perhaps to be achieved over several years. Of course, one would have to revise that at the time of new negotiations, but the magnitude would certainly be very large.

Question: You mentioned the possibility of using surplus OPEC funds in this new recycling-substitution account. Would this not be injecting liquidity and inflationary pressures into the system, since it would really monetize the OPEC surpluses immediately rather than over a longer time period, and would channel the funds to the countries that are most likely to spend them immediately?

Answer: I have assumed that in any case there is a recycling need that must be satisfied. In the near future it may be difficult to do all of the recycling through existing channels and, therefore, to augment the present system with this new mechanism would strengthen the international monetary system.

Question: It seems that a fundamental constraint on all of the SDR substitution-account schemes is that they must have a yield at least as high as reserve holders could obtain in private markets. If so, then will not these funds become very expensive for the deficit countries that will be borrowing them? How can you make a substitution account simultaneously attractive to both lenders and borrowers?

Answer: I do not feel that the SDR assets must have a yield at least as high as is available in private markets because I think an advantage of the SDR is that the exchange risk is less with this diversified asset. Of course, central banks may feel that they can do better if they always choose the best currency. I think, however, that the consensus should have to develop that central banks have responsibility for the functioning of the international monetary system and not for making profits.

**Part II
The Role of
Commercial Banks
in LDC Finance in
the 1980s**

4 Government Policies and Economic Growth in Developing Countries

Kurt Richebacher

My remarks are rather brief because everything I have to say concerns a few fundamentals that are always the same for every country, whether highly or less developed, whether in external surplus or deficit, whether market or planned economy. The basic condition for economic growth is that there must be sufficient capital formation and investment for full employment. Economic theory once began with the question of capital accumulation.

In the long run, rising employment and rising real incomes do not simply depend on monetary demand but on the enlargement of the productive equipment of a country. Economic growth ultimately depends on how much the people in a country are able or willing to save and to invest and how much of their real resources they use for consumption. As the classical economists liked to say: Industry is limited by capital, though, admittedly, production does not always come up to that limit. Where and when unused resources of all kinds exist, the operation of this principle, obviously, is temporarily suspended. Nevertheless, when we think of long-run development the rate of investment is the central problem of a sound employment and growth policy. It is clear that men equipped with machines produce more than men equipped with simple tools. However, to have these machines a community must release sufficient resources for the maintenance, improvement, and enlargment of its capital equipment.

In other words, economic-growth theory as well as employment theory are capital theory and nothing else. Capital formation is the vital variable in the economic development of a country. But if we want to understand capital theory and ultimately the fundamental conditions for economic growth, we must think in physical terms and not in monetary terms. The real problems lie below the monetary surface, and they cannot be solved by financial gadgets. In order to understand today's situation, that is the present decline in economic growth and employment in conjunction with so much higher inflation rates, it is important to realize the pernicious effects of fiscal and monetary policies on the allocation of resources between investments and consumption.

Whenever I try to check the economic health of a country, I turn first to the GNP statistics. How great a proportion of total GNP is devoted to real capital formation? The larger it is, that is, the larger the part of current products retained for investment, the higher the rate of economic growth that can be generated. Low capital-formation proportions mean low rates of growth of national product, unless more output can be turned out per unit of capital. Then my question is: Are there any marked changes in the use of resources, and in what direction? Though I am aware of the fact that there is nothing like a fixed technical relationship between capital input and incremental rise in output, it appears safe to assume as a rule that economic growth will increase if the ratio within the investment national product rises, and conversely, that growth will go downhill if that ratio shrinks.

There is a lot of talk lately, particularly in the United States, about supply-side economics in contrast with Keynesian-demand management. In fact, I have some diffculty in placing these advocates of so-called supply-side economics within my building of economic theories. It strikes me as very Keynesian when I hear these newborn supply economists speak of nothing else but of the incentives they want to provide in order to get higher productive investment, as if lack of incentives or lack of demand for investible resources were the only or certainly the governing limiting factor of present investment activity. Never a single word is heard about possible limits to capital formation on the supply side in the sense of an eventual shortage of available real resources not permitting higher investment in the first place. Needless to say, this same question has to be posed with respect to capital exports to developing countries, meaning capital exports not in the sense of lending money but in the sense of lending and transferring real capital resources, the aim of these transfers being to add to the generally insufficient internal capital formation of these countries.

This way of looking at things in real terms throws light on our terrible failures as well as on the failures of so many of these countries. Amongst them we see all sorts of economies, some fully planned with socialist systems, some part way or full way to capitalism and free markets, and some still predominantly feudal. But never mind these differences in political and economic systems, their central problem is everywhere exactly the same: in order to raise output and living standards they need capital, capital, and still more capital—including corresponding know-how, of course. Considering fuılieı tlial tliese developing countries have an overall population growth on average of 2.5 percent per annum, it is obvious that they need a tremendous amount of capital simply to maintain their living standards.

It is easy to see that this problem of capital exports from the industrial countries to the LDCs has two sides that need to be examined. One concerns the capacity of the industrial nations to export surplus investable resources, meaning resources in excess of the requirements for their own economic growth, and the other concerns the capacity of the developing countries to absorb imported foreign capital in a useful way. There is strong presumption that there must be limits to this too.

Now, speaking of capital and capital formation has its great difficulties in our time, because both these terms are shrouded in great ambiguity. To avoid any possibly confusion, let met, therefore, stress one distinction of absolutely crucial importance: the distinction between bits of paper, all coming from the printing press, like money, government bonds, or Special Drawing Rights, for example, and the realities of capital in the form of productive plant and equipment on the one hand, and the realities of capital formation, representing the current additions to the real capital stock already in existence, on the other hand.

It is necessary at this point to clarify still another misconception that is held not only by the public but also by many professional economists. All industrial countries now have considerable overcapacities of plant in a great many industries. From this undoubted fact the conclusion is wrongly drawn that we have too much capital, that we have indeed saved too much and would be much better off if we would spend a larger fraction of our incomes. Nothing could be further from the truth. The worsening of growth performance and prospects in the industrial countries and consequently in the rest of the world has one ultimate and deep-seated cause: excess consumption at the expense of capital formation, that is, a growing shortage of capital.

We have not overinvested during these last ten years, we have underinvested, and we have underinvested not because we consume too little but because our demand for consumption goods and services has become too high, too pressing, too absorbing. This growing pressure in the direction of higher consumption and not the oil price rises is at the root of the gradual slowing down in the dynamism of all industrial countries with which we are visibly confronted. Our dynamism has gone with the wind of our investment power, and our investment power has gone with the wind of economic policies that everywhere aimed at one and the same thing: to throw more and more real resources into the service of current consumption. Contrary to some beliefs, however, those resources added to the consumption sphere did not fall from heaven. What we actually did was to increase consumption at the expense of investment, and the necessary level of accumulation cannot be maintained.

The mechanism by which such a conversion of national economy works is the system of relative prices and costs. The increased nominal purchasing power in the hands of consumers and the public sector forces the prices of labor and materials to higher levels where they become too expensive for profitable production. Firms producing capital goods geared to unprofitable productive investment find that they face increased factor costs while demand for their machines is falling off. Hence these firms contract, while others producing goods and services for the consumer that are adapted to the changed structure of demand find demand rising and increase their ouput. However, even though governments, consumers, and the corresponding industries surely gain in the short run, they also will suffer in the long run, because the falling rate of capital accumulation is bound to reduce total incomes in the future below what they would otherwise be.

Needless to say, these policies are most damaging to the industrial countries themselves in the first place. Yet, the destruction of investment power and economic growth is not merely detrimental to themselves but also to the rest of the world, especially developing countries that are very much dependent on the capacity of the developed countries to import consumption goods and to export capital. As a result of our economic policies we shall more and more fail in our duty on both accounts. Many people think that the industrial countries do their duty to the world by simply spending themselves into current-account deficits. It hurts me to listen to such short-sighted economics. Just compare the records of different countries; look at those that first complied with this recipe of overspending: Great Britain and the United States, which long ago lost their dynamism, if ever they possessed it. To the discomfiture of Keynesian model builders, countries like Japan, Germany, and the common-market nations took over the role of the dynamic focus of the world economy. Fast increases in productivity in these countries were combined with, or resulted in, a highly positive balance of payment on current account, about which there were endless complaints. But as these countries grew more rapidly, so did their imports, much faster in any case than the imports of the countries geared to low savings and high consumption.

Can there be any doubt that rapid growth and progress in these countries was more beneficial to the rest of the world, in spite of any accruing export surplus, than the weak-growth performance of the high life and high spending countries that constantly see themselves compelled to implement stop-and-go policies. At the same time, the export surpluses produced by the fast-growing countries represented a genuine source of capital exports in the sense of lending and transferring real resources to other countries. I completely fail to understand, however, how a deficit country that, by definition, spends more than it produces, can ever be a true capital exporter, except an exporter of money and inflation. Such a balance of payments renders lending of capital to foreign countries impossible without causing a devaluation. I wonder very much about German capital exports.

As for the developing countries, to be quite frank, when I read about the torrid pace at which their external debts pile up, I wonder what is being financed with these credits. The deficit country, clearly, is absorbing more, taking consumption and investment together, than its own production; in a sense it is drawing upon savings made abroad. In return it incurs an obligation to pay interest or profits at the expense of future proceeds, and thus, at the expense of the future import potential. Whether this is a good bargain or not depends on the nature of the use to which the borrowed funds and resources are put. If they merely permit an excess of consumption over production the economy is on the road to ruin.

Characteristic feature of virtually all less-developed countries are a dearth of capital and a relative abundance of land and labor. The scarcity of capital reflects an inability to generate adequate domestic savings. External capital inflows are supposed to supplement domestic savings and, at the same time, provide the borrower with scarce foreign exchange. Most developing planning models concerned with the role of foreign aid in underdeveloped economies assume that external resources add to the overall availability of savings, without in any way substituting for savings made available from domestic sources.

During the last years we have read a lot about the great recycling job, done by the international banking system. In my opinion, considering world inflation, we clearly had overcycling, overlending, and overborrowing. I have more than serious doubts about the capacity of most developing countries to absorb resources for productive purpose in any sensible relation to these unbelievable international credit flows. If so, the upshot of this financing can only be to give support to consumption at levels that cannot be sustained. Rather than accelerating growth, this relative excess consumption can only retard it in the long run.

Trying to check the validity of this presumption or suspicion, I have gone through some international reports, looking for confirmation or refutation. Unfortunately, I found much more of the former than of the latter. The report of the Inter-American Development Bank was most helpful. It is a report that I can only recommend for reading, because the authors analyze country by country shifts in the use of gross national product. What is rising as a percentage of gross domestic product? It is government expenditure, private consumption, or capital formation, that is, real investment?

To summarize, in 1978, the last year under report available to me, current expenditures increased more than capital expenditures in most Latin American countries. Government expenditures on goods and services constitute the largest part of current expenditure in all Latin American countries except Brazil and Colombia. During that year, the overall fiscal deficit of fourteen central governments was higher as a percentage of gross domestic product (GDP) than the average of the preceeding five years, while capital formation decreased as a share of total expenditures. In fact, capital expenditures fell noticeably. Only four countries—Bahamas, Guatemala, Paraguay, and Uruguay—were successful in allocating an increasing proportion of fiscal resources to capital formation while simultaneously increasing relative savings and improving their overall deficit position.

5 American Banks and Developing Countries' Financial Needs

William B. Eagleson, Jr.

This chapter considers the specific role of U.S. banks in lending to developing nations both now and in the years immediately ahead. The challenge in discussing this subject is apparent in view of a dilemma. On the one hand, it appears that international banking lending will not and cannot continue to grow as rapidly as in the past five years. On the other hand, most agree that private banks will be required to make a further contribution if serious frictions are to be avoided in future extensive recycling tasks.

Two general introductory remarks are called for. First, the terms LDC, third world, and so on are of course imprecise, as is the thought that the name OPEC adequately describes all oil-producing nations. In the context of this chapter LDC and like terms should be understood to refer to low-income capital-deficit nations, even though as in the case of Indonesia, for example, they may be petroleum exporters. The terms LDC and third world include Yugoslavia, but not Poland and other centrally planned economies.

Second, it is immediately evident that financing of the developing world cannot be discussed except in the context of the recycling problem, which has assumed a new and enlarged dimension following the second oil shock. Indeed, the question of bank involvement in this process is of interest only as part of a larger issue: is our institutional structure as a whole adequate for recycling on the scale that seems likely to be required?

A measure of the potential problem can be found in the fact that after five years of stability at a level of about $30 billion, the aggregate current-account deficit of non-OPEC LDC nations has doubled in two years to perhaps $65 billion in 1980. Estimates for 1981 center around $75 billion.

I intend to consider first the present position of U.S. banks in the spectrum of bank lending to the developing world and then the changes that can be foreseen in this position. Finally, I am prompted by my own orientation and by some recently published examples of what seem to me to be wishful thinking on the subject to conclude with brief special attention to the role of the regional U.S. banks.

Bank financing of payments deficits and of third-world development, as contrasted with financing through bond issues, had its origins after World War II and its coming of age only in the last fifteen years or so. By the time of the first oil shock in 1973, developing nations' external indebtedness to banks probably had not reached $30 billion in total. During the remainder of the decade of the 1970s, however, bank-held debt rose five-fold in response to several different forces.

The combined impact of a quadrupling of oil prices and recession in certain industrialized countries had a devastating effect on developing nations' economies and their payments balances. The resulting deficits were funded jointly by official institutions and by commercial banks. The latter, competing both for market share and for stature in world banking, have remained willing lenders after a relatively brief pause at the time of the Herstatt crisis.

U.S. banks have been in the forefront of this lending to the developing world, and as recently as 1976 they held more than half of all the bank debt of those countries. At year-end, 1979 Federal Reserve Board figures show total bank claims on nonoil developing nations of almost $150 billion. U.S. banks held some $55 billion of that total, or about 38 percent.

It should be noted in passing that the claims are highly concentrated among relatively few lenders. The World Bank has estimated that only thirty banks hold half of the $150 billion total of bank claims, and the firm of Salomon Brothers has calculated that the ten largest U.S. banks hold three-quarters of the $55 billion held by U.S. banks in total.

The prominence of U.S. banks in third-world-lending has at least two possible explanations. First, virtually all such credits were denominated in U.S. dollars until relatively recently. Thus among the variety of risks involved, those of exchange-rate variation and dollar availability could be avoided only by the U.S. institutions that were operating in their own currency. The ready access of foreign banks to U.S. dollar deposits in the Euromarkets has of course removed this obstacle in more recent years.

Second, the more rapidly growing domestic economies may have occupied the attention of large German and Japanese banks, for example, after their U.S. competitors had begun to look abroad to satisfy lending appetites.

Whether differing regulatory attitudes affected the timing or speed of entry into LDC lending by the banking instituions of the several industrialized nations is not clear. It is more certain that regulatory attitudes concerning capital adequacy, country risk levels, and concentrations of exposure have contributed to the recent decline in the share of this market which is held by U.S. banks.

In summary, the risks and techniques of LDC lending were explored and charted by U.S. banks, and these institutions dominated the market until about 1978. Although their dollar exposure has continued to grow, market share has eroded to something less than 40 percent recently.

Let us now turn to a closer consideration of the forces behind this trend that seem likely to dictate the role of the U.S. banks in the years immediately ahead. A combination of factors, some of which are defined and measurable and some of which are more subjective, suggest that U.S. banks will play a reduced role in future LDC financing. This does not necessarily indicate a decline or even a leveling in total dollar exposures, but rather a falling off in market share of U.S. institutions, leaving more to foreign banks and to international official institutions.

The first groups of forces includes the various empirical controls of risk, liquidity, and exposure concentration that are imposed by law, regulation, or an individual bank's own management judgment. LDC lending, although not free of credit risk by any means, involves a variety of political and social judgments as well. Since a high proportion of such lending is to government entities or is guaranteed by governments, lending decisions involve an assessment of country risk.

In observing the ancient bankers' dictum to avoid concentrations of risk, country or house limits are established by banks involved in this business that limit exposure on a country-by-country basis. Because of the rapid growth in external bank-held debt of nations such as Brazil and Mexico, many U.S. banks are approaching self-imposed limits on exposure in these countries with the result that future lending must more nearly match the runoff of existing debt.

A similar constraint is imposed by U.S. bank capital ratios. Most of the loan growth of U.S. money-center banks in the last decade has been international, and if balance-sheet strain should require a slowdown in lending it is likely to be in that area.

Wilfried Guth in his remarks to the International Monetary Conference in New Orleans this spring pointed to the declining capital ratios of the large U.S. banks, noting that they are among the most highly leveraged in the world. Such data is not necessarily meaningful by itself and must be viewed in the context of a national banking system's involvement with government. Nevertheless, capital ratios are one of the measurement tools used by U.S. bank regulators, and it is probable that they will serve to limit the growth of international loan portfolios in particular for at least the next several years.

A second set of factors affecting the future role of U.S. banks' LDC lending is of a prudential nature and is judgmental rather than strictly quantifiable. It involves the attitudes of analysts, of funds suppliers, of the press and, not least, of bank management itself about levels of risk and opportunity in third-world lending.

Banks' credit experience in foreign lending has been very good. Although there have been several instances of what is generally described as debt restructuring, there have been no repudiations of bank-held sovereign-risk debt in recent years. At the same time it is clear that recent world developments have greatly heightened the risks involved in international lending. The most obvious of these are a malfunctioning world monetary system, the prospect of chronic energy shortages, and the associated change in the process of oil-price determination.

The combination of these forces has created conditions in which at least some developing nations are unable to repay debt except with the proceeds of new borrowing. Further, heightened political risk is perceived in some countries, adding to the general concern about risk levels in LDC lending.

The response of bankers to such developments is to limit exposure in order to forestall doubts on the part of funds suppliers and others about their institution's soundness. Public confidence directly affects both the cost and the availability of funding. Sensitivity to this most fragile of bank assets is a more powerful incentive to caution and prudence than is regulatory sanction. In any case, both official and prudential pressures are in concert at the moment, producing a climate in which loans to developing nations will grow considerably less rapidly than they have in the past decade.

The discussion thus far has addressed the roles of perhaps fifteen large U.S. money-center banks that account for less than half of all U.S. bank deposits but for perhaps 80 percent of U.S. bank lending to LDCs in total. The dilemma presented by recycling requirements and the limited extent to which it appears that these and other large banks can fill the expected gap in recycling capacity have caused some to propose a larger role for the regional or second-tier U.S. banks. The World Bank, for example, in its *World Development Report 1980,* observes the following: "Second-tier banks that are comparatively underlent relative to their capital will probably expand their international lending, but because these banks are smaller, less experienced, and probably more risk-averse than the large international lenders, developing countries are likely to pay more for their services."

This suggestion is appealing since the remainder of the top fifty U.S. banks represent a pool of lending capacity one-third the size of the money-center institutions. There are several reasons, however, why a significantly larger role in lending to developing nations seems unlikely for the second-tier institutions.

First, and perhaps most compelling, the profit margins recently available in LDC lending are simply not attractive to most regional banks. These institutions on average earn 50 percent more on each dollar of assets than do the money-center institutions. Average gross spreads on Eurocurrency lending before allocation of operating costs, taxes, or provisions for loan-loss reserves are now barely equal to the margins being earned by the regional banks. Net spreads after adjusting for those costs are not sufficient to maintain current margins of the regional institutions.

Salomon Brothers has calculated that the average spread over LIBOR (London Interbank Offer Rate) in Eurocurrency lending, not all of which is to LDCs, fell from 1.52 percent in 1976 to 0.76 percent last year, roughly three-quarters of one percent. It is interesting to observe also that over the same period the average maturity of new loans rose from 5.75 years to 9 years.

It is not necessary here to examine the reasons for the narrowing of spreads; one can readily visualize a reverse trend under pressures of market considerations already discussed. Also, as Henry Wallich has pointed out, as LIBOR rises the spread required to sustain a desired return on equity tends to fall. Still, it seems likely that this market will have only marginal appeal to the relatively more profitable second-tier lenders.

The fifteen largest U.S. banks that constitute the money-center institutions and that have been preeminent in LDC lending find these narrow spreads acceptable because the marketplace allows them a leverage or a gearing sufficient to generate a reasonable return on equity, even on lower return-on-asset levels. For the remainder of the top fifty U.S. banks, the major regionals, it is evident that a much higher return on assets, and thus lending spreads, is necessary in order to achieve a similar result. Third-world lending does not at present offer the required margins without concentrations of risk or exposure, or both.

A further deterrent to the acceptance of an enlarged lending role by second-tier banks lies in the fact that few, if any, of these institutions have a corporate-strategy commitment to the developing world that might provide an incentive to build or even maintain a presence through a cycle of risk or rate spreads. Without a strategic role among LDCs, faced with narrow spreads, lengthening maturities, and a heightened level of risk, and without the benefit of fee income enjoyed by the large syndicators, the second-tier bank is likely to reduce and not to build its relative exposure in this particular field of lending.

To summarize these remarks, in the five years following the initial oil schock in 1973 the current-account deficit of nonoil LDCs remained around $30 billion annually, and the international financial community led by the commercial banks proved capable of handling the funding. Subsequent oil-price adjustments, however, have resulted in a doubling of third-world deficits to a level around $65 billion this year, and further significant increases are forecast for the years immediately ahead.

Deep concerns are being voiced about the ability of the existing machinery to recycle OPEC surpluses, currently exceeding $100 billion and growing, to deficit nations generally and particularly to the LDCs.

At present, commercial banks in developed nations are funding something more than half of the LDC deficits, but for a number of reasons it is unlikely that the larger deficits expected in the 1980s can be dealt with by increased bank lending, particularly on the part of the U.S. institutions. In many cases, exposures to individual countries already approach limits dictated by regulation or judgment. Also, capital constraints and a heightened level of risk in international lending will tend to limit increases in exposure.

Suggestions that second-tier banks may assume a larger share of the burden appear to overlook the obstacles of high profit margins and lower levels of risk tolerance among these institutions.

If, then, we face a period in which recycling requirements will escalate and the appetite of U.S. banks for LDC loans fails to grow, how then will the shortfall be made up? There appear to me to be three possibilities.

First, there could be increased lending by non-U.S. banks. Although these institutions are already providing nearly 65 percent of the total bank recycling credit, there may still be room for further increase.

A second possibility lies in increased lending by official institutions, a subject Johannes Witteveen discusses in chapter 3 of this book. There are some political and legal problems, as he pointed out, but larger roles for both the World Bank and the International Monetary Fund seem to me to be likely.

A third possibility is direct lending by OPEC. This is the essential ingredient in any solution that is to be more than a temporary one.

A final element in the adjustment process, however, looms larger and more potentially destructive to developed nations and to LDCs alike with each new increase in oil prices. That element of course is the prospect of a reduction in LDC deficits achieved through forced reductions in their living standards. A central question of our time is whether ways can be found to avoid that particular result.

6 Private versus Official Sources of Finance for Developing Countries

Koei Narusawa

LDC financing by international commercial banks is by no means a new phenomenon. Its history dates as far back as the early postwar period. There is no denying the fact, however, that this issue was heightened by the first oil crisis that occured in late 1973. In retrospect, the widespread disequilibrium of balance of payments within the global context, which at first appeared devastating to the entire world economy, was resolved without causing unbearable side effects. This was due partly to the unexpectedly high degree of absorptive capacities on the part of the OPEC countries, which resulted in the rapid decline in their balance-of-payments surplus. On the other hand, one must not underestimate the intermediary role played by the international banking system in recycling the petrodollars to the deficit countries.

The second oil crisis in early 1979 again brought about a situation similar to what had obtained after the first one. This time around, however, the circumstances surrounding the international banking system are undoubtedly more unfavorable than during the previous time. First, a number of oil-importing countries, particularly those in the third world, are already heavily indebted as a result of heavy foreign borrowing in the preceding years. Second, capital adequacy had come to constrain the lending capacity of the international banks. Third, the portfolio concentration on specific countries set limitations to the scope for expansion of banks' additional commitments to the countries concerned. Last, a growing awareness on the part of banks of the so-called country risk is also worth noting as an additional factor constraining the lending policy of the banks toward specific countries whose credibility is deemed questionable.

Despite all these adverse factors the external deficit of nonoil LDCs has thus far been financed smoothly, partly by drawing down external reserves built up in the preceding years, and partly by drawing upon unused facilities arranged previously. The major contribution is this regard, however, is again being made by the commercial banking system, which has proved its high degree of resilience. The real test, however, will come in 1981 and beyond, because deficit financing through private banking channels can by no means be continued indefinitely in the same manner as has been done.

There are a number of significant points worth mentioning. First, there will be a growing need for the deficit countries, particularly those in the third world, to press forward with an adjustment process of their own balance of payments, which should ideally be facilitated by the assistance to be provided by multilateral financial institutions such as the World Bank and the IMF. In this connection, it was an encouraging step in the right direction that the World Bank introduced a new scheme of program loans to meet these requirements on the part of nonoil LDCs.

Second, surplus countries should also be encouraged to actively participate in the recycling process by stepping up their direct financial assistance to the nonoil LDCs. Such a direct-recycling process, albeit highly desirable, is admittedly subject to relatively strict quantitative limitations, since the surplus countries are not prepared to take on the unlimited credit risks involved because their surpluses are being built up as a result of exchange of their own unrenewable resources for unwanted dollars, and they are naturally interested in maintaining the capital value of their financial assets thus accumulated.

Such being the case, the MDIs will have to play an enhanced role as intermediaries for the recycling of petrodollars in the years immediately ahead of us. One of the ways of achieving the objective will be the wider use of cofinancing facilities with the World Bank and other MDIs operating on a regional basis. Furthermore, these MDIs may possibly be able to assist commercial banks in getting easier access to information vital to the proper credit evaluation on the part of lenders. The most important role to be played by the IMF in strengthening the recycling process is no doubt the full utilization of its expanded lending capacity by securing additional ways and means for its funding operations. So far as I am informed, additional funds required for 1981 are estimated to be in the region of SDR six to seven billion. This computation is said to be based on the standby agreements already entered into or under negotiation at present. One of the major ways of additional funding by the IMF will be the direct placement by the IMF with the surplus countries, Saudi Arabia in particular. This new channel will most probably have to be supplemented by the IMF's direct borrowing in a similar fashion from industrial countries.

Should the direct borrowing both from OPEC and from the industrial countries prove to be insufficient to meet the requirements, borrowing by the IMF from private markets will have to be given due consideration as another alternative for its funding operations. We commercial bankers would in principle be prepared to accept the IMF as a prime borrower. It will nevertheless be highly advisable for the Fund to enter into the private markets in a prudential manner. This applies both to the magnitude of its borrowing and to the pace at which it proceeds with borrowing. It is true that a certain amount of fear has been expressed regarding the possibility of the so-called crowding out in case the IMF enters into private markets as a new entrant. The fear of such a crowding-out, however, is ill founded. In fact, I would expect the desired additionality to be achieved by the IMF's entry into private markets.

Regarding the Fund's lending activities, much criticism has been voiced about the stringency of the so-called conditionality the Fund usually attaches to the credit facilities extended to member countries. By means of this conditionality the Fund is able to perform a sort of watchdog function. I do not identify myself with the idea of relaxing the conditionality too far, let alone eliminating it altogether. There is no denying, however, that the conventional notion of the Fund's conditionality is due for modification in order to comply with the changed nature of balance-of-payments deficits in the wake of the oil crisis.

I am among a great number of commercial bankers who believe in the high standard of resiliency and capability of commercial banks as intermediaries of the international flow of capital—even under the forseeable bleak circumstances. In this context, however, one should not treat the nonoil LDCs as a single group of countries; rather, we have to distinguish those relatively high-income countries enjoying higher credit ratings from those relatively low-income LDCs in particular, whose creditworthiness is questioned according to the standards set by commercial banks. The latter group of LDCs undoubtedly has to be taken care of in the main by official institutions with concessional terms and conditions.

Two proposals regarding the further reinforcement of the existing recycling mechanism deserve special attention. One is the proposed energy affiliate of the World Bank. In view of the fact that the development of energy resources calls for enormous capital, the investment risks involved will be too great to be borne by private institutions alone. There exist, however, a number of developing countries that are endowed with potential energy resources waiting for exploration and development. In this sense, establishment of a new international institution like the one proposed by Robert McNamara would be highly desirable. The other proposal calls for the introduction of an additional international insurance scheme with a view to covering a part of the credit risk involved in the lending to LDCs. This concept will be particularly useful for so-called threshold countries whose credibility falls barely short of the standards set by commercial considerations. Equally important will be the efforts on the part of the industrial world to provide easier and broader access to their own domestic markets for LDCs desirous of promoting their nontraditional exports to the developed world.

Let me conclude by saying that it is my sincere hope that the new Reagan administration all prove to be outward-looking enough to provide due support to the matter of international economic and financial cooperation in order to successfully cope with the recycling problem.

Discussion

Question: How it is possible to achieve an increase in the share of investment without some reduction in living standards in the developing countries, especially in light of high oil prices? If it is not possible, then how does the internal adjustment unfold in the context of political realities?

Answer: You cannot reconcile the two. You can increase consumption in the short run by throwing resources into consumption at the expense of capital formation, and that is what we all have been doing over the last ten years. But in every country which does this you have falling consumption in the long run. For example, the German government has thrown 5 percent of GNP out of investment and into government consumption, and this has cut the growth rate in half.

In the short run, it is necessary to lower living standards in order to have higher rates of capital formation but, of course, it pays in the long run. However, politicians and, unfortunately, too many of their advisors, believe in the short-run methods to increase consumption. I wonder where our growth rates will be in ten years, since most countries have cut their growth rate in half over the last ten years.

Question: Could not the nonoil LDCs help themselves with the capital accumulation problem by creating an environment that would encourage both domestic capital accumulation and capital inflows—not loans, but simply profitable businesslike capital inflows?

Answer: Brazil has used the inflationary system to redistribute income toward capital formation, and they have had a very high capital-formation ratio. Eventually, however, almost all governments have to ease up and allow consumption to increase. For example, Brazil recently did just this, and as a result investment in Brazil has almost collapsed.

Question: I must confess some confusion as to what the incentives would be for developing countries to cooperate with the solutions that have been suggested. One is to spread the risk of international lending by involving the development banks and the IMF, the other is a structural adjustment by the developing countries. The LDCs presumably do not want to borrow from the IMF because of conditionality; that is why they have been borrowing from private banks. Also, presumably, the LDCs do not want some kind of structural adjustment because there are strong domestic pressures that force the governments into policies of overconsumption. Would any of you like to comment on this?

Answer 1: If the existing sources of funds are not sufficient for the task to be performed, then the borrowing nations are going to have to go where the money is. They will be forced to accept whatever conditions the lenders may wish to set. That is the incentive—simple need.

Answer 2: The international banking system has neglected the question of seeing to it that the funds lent to the developing countries are really used in a structural way, which will help them in the long run. If you finance overconsumption, it looks quite nice in the short run, but you are in trouble in the long run.

Answer 3: There will be a need on the part of the borrowing LDCs to help themselves by rectifying their balance-of-payments structures. The adjustment process is one way to deal with the entire problem. Deficit financing will not solve the problem. As I said during my presentation, however, the adjustment process might be rather painful for many countries, and, thus, they will need the help of the advanced countries by means of international institutions such as the IMF and the World Bank.

Answer 4: One thing is clear. These problems of capital accumulation and overconsumption are independent of the oil-price increases. The fact is that you could argue that the oil price rises mean an increase in saving in the world, since the oil money comes out of our income and, thus, our consumption is reduced. In other words, the oil sheiks are reducing our living standard, and their savings can theoretically be borrowed and used to increase world investment. All this makes sense, but when you examine the facts, you see that we are really maintaining consumption and reducing investment.

Question: The facts that I hear do not fit together in the way that I see the world. First, we learn that loans to developing countries are becoming increasingly risky. It should (1) tend to make their rates of return rise, and (2) their rates of return should be higher than those on less risky domestic loans. However, we are told that one potential source of funds for the LDCs is the second-tier banks in the United States, but that the rate of return on such loans is too low to allow these banks to enter the international money market. If these loans are risky and if we anticipate a shortfall, why isn't their rate of return high enough to entice new lenders into the market? Second, what is there about the international money market that makes us concerned that the market will not clear? In other words, why do we worry about a shortage of funds, if interest rates can move freely to equate supply and demand?

Answer 1: I do not know why the decline in spreads has occurred on loans that bear an escalated level of risk. One possible answer may be that bankers have been forced to accept whatever spreads the borrowers have been able to negotiate, and these spreads have been coming down. Also, Henry Wallich has made a very interesting point that many bankers do not readily grasp: that at higher and higher levels of LIBOR the spreads needed to maintain a given return on equity tend to decline. Thus, the declining spreads to some extent exaggerate the impact on bank profitability.

Answer 2: I am of the opinion that the existing spread on international lending is not quite sufficient to cover the risk involved in the lending to

LDCs. However, this is more or less decided by market forces. Recently, the demand for loans in the advanced countries is very depressed as a result of the worldwide recession. Thus, the market conditions tend to be in favor of the LDC borrowers, despite the fact that the creditworthiness of the borrowing countries has been deteriorating.

Question: Recognizing the realities of the 1980s, should not the OPEC cartel be fully included as a partner in any negotiations on monetary matters? Should we not attempt to link the price of oil and the price of capital? And, should we not work toward a mechanism that would provide some assurance for OEPC capital around the world in return for assurances of a more secure supply of oil from the Middle East?

Answer: I do not know whether the OPEC countries can be persuaded by us, but certainly we are not even trying to pursue a sensible policy by which they could be persuaded.

7 Central Bank Intervention and Cooperation

Henry Wallich

Intervention in the foreign-exchange markets by monetary authorities is a general practice and, on balance, has contributed to the smooth functioning of the international monetary system since generalized floating of exchange rates began in 1973. It requires a great deal of cooperation among monetary authorities, which has been forthcoming. Without claiming perfection, intervention has been a positive force, and, in that sense, one of the modest success stories of these difficult years.

Nevertheless, there is little that is systematic about foreign-exchange market intervention. Many countries have their own styles of intervening. Some rules were developed by the IMF and its offspring, the Committee of Twenty, in 1974. With the adoption of the Second Amendment to the IMF Articles of Agreement, the IMF in 1977 laid down some principles for the guidance of members' exchange-rate policies. To date, however, the IMF's involvement in this area has not gone much beyond generalities. There is no effort at present to codify or systematize intervention activity, other than among the members of the European Monetary System in their exchange-market relations with each other.

Intervention activity in most countries is sporadic and unplanned, reflecting disturbances in exchange markets as they occur. The scale on which it occurs has varied from nominal to many billions over periods of a few months, usually without the authorities being able to tell in advance what the scale would be.

In the early days of floating, there was concern among some observers that monetary authorities might operate at cross purposes in the exchange market. It was feared that some countries might want their currencies to appreciate or depreciate, which might have pitted their monetary authorities against each other in the exchange markets. That was one reason why the IMF tried its hand at devising guidelines for floating. In fact, there have been few operations at cross purposes. That is not to say that exchange rates have always moved in an agreed direction or have behaved in a stabilizing way. But the interventions of monetary authorities in the exchange markets have almost without exception been consistent rather than conflicting.

There are two principal reasons for this. First, the major countries have not had precise exchange-rate objectives. The problem of making such rate objectives consistent, therefore, has for the most part not arisen. Second, monetary authorities have abstained from aggressive intervention, that is, from driving the rate by pushing it in a direction in which it was already moving. Intervention has been in the form of leaning against the wind, seeking to slow down whatever movement the market produced in either direction, without reducing the movement to zero and thereby capping or pegging a rate. It is not a really significant exception to the general observance of this rule when the monetary authorities of countries diversifying out of the dollar have sold dollars on the way down and bought deutsche marks (DM), Swiss francs, and yen on the way up. Typically, the currencies of diversifiers are not floating currencies and are not involved in that sense. The injunction against aggressive intervention is one of the 1974 IMF guidelines that has survived in practice and has stood us in good stead. Of course, countries can and do influence exchange rates by means other than intervention, such as through interest rates and through other policies influencing the balance of payments and the relative performance of their economies. But the role of intervention has been kept limited.

In any particular instance, there may still be ambiguities. For example, are continued central-bank purchases of a currency appropriate when the currency is weak during the early part of the market day but turns around in the course of the day, perhaps in a different time zone? It is appropriate for a country whose currency is weak to moderate the decline by selling dollars while the dollar itself is weakening against third currencies? In most cases, the answer would probably be yes, but there might be differences of view. Since there is no judge to adjudicate cases, the answer is in the hands of the cooperating monetary authorities.

Cooperation, based on continuous contract and consultation, is particularly important where markets for the same currencies are located in different time zones. If traders were able to spot significantly different policies with respect to, for example, dollar/DM intervention in Frankfurt and New York, during their respective market hours, perhaps they could make money out of it. The appearance of different purposes in different markets would be disturbing to trades in any event. It is important that efforts to prevent such situations continue to be attended by success.

Exchange-Rate Preferences

Exchange-market intervention policies reflect a country's preferences with respect to exchange rates. Even though most countries, whose currencies are floating, do not have specific exchange-rate objectives, they usually do have preferences. In most cases, nowadays, monetary authorities prefer their own currency to be strong, so long as it is not driven to levels that makes them uncompetitive in trade. This reflects the concern, universal among central banks, with the danger of inflation. A strong currency holds down the cost of imports, thereby reducing inflationary pressure. The opposite attitude, aiming at competitive depreciation as a means of stimulating exports and employment, nowadays is not a persuasive objective. There are other means, if needed, to promote employment than by debasement of the national currency.

This attitude is apparent from the frequent statements of policymakers. It is observable also from the fact that on balance countries tend to support their own currency when it is weak more readily and on a larger scale than to hold it down when it is strong and the dollar is weak. During periods of pronounced market trends, such as the decline of the dollar in 1977 and 1978, efforts to mitigate the decline of the dollar were widespread.

Countries are restrained in the pursuit of their exchange-rate preferences and, therefore, in the extent of their intervention by monetary-policy considerations. Intervention to moderate the appreciation of the home currency leads to the creation of bank reserves and additional money supply. These operations, therefore, are potentially inflationary, unless offset by monetary-policy action that sterilizes the expansion. Most countries find it relatively easy to absorb bank excess reserves created through intervention by the sale of short-term paper to the banks or through increases in reserve requirements. They often find it difficult to sterilize the increase in the money supply because that would require a positive contraction of bank credit if done by way of the banking system. The alternative technique—sale of short-term paper to nonbanks—is not open to most countries because they lack a market for such instruments among nonbanks. The United States, with its wide market for short-term government and other paper among individuals, corporations, and institutional investors, has a distinct advantage in this regard. Encouragement of similar markets in other countries would enhance the capability of those countries' monetary authorities to intervene in exchange markets.

Another area of monetary policy that interacts with intervention policy is interest rates. Exchange rates are responsive to interest rates, and the objectives of intervention can also be accomplished by appropriate changes in interest rates, although not on a day-by-day basis. Interest-rate changes that would favorably affect the exchange rate may not be desirable, however, from the point of view of domestic monetary policy. In such a situation, it may be tempting for a central bank to substitute intervention, sterilized if possible, for interest-rate action. Alternatively, intervention may be employed to offset an interest-rate action taken for domestic reasons that is positively destabilizing to exchange rates. However, the volume of intervention that might be needed to accomplish these purposes could easily mount very rapidly. Accordingly, it seems to be the general view of monetary authorities that intervention can be employed as a substitute for interest-rate movements only to a very limited extent.

Recently, interest rates in the United States have become more volatile as a result of the more rigorous reserve-based operating technique of the Federal Reserve. This has contributed also, in some degree, to greater volatility in dollar exchange rates. Under these circumstances, it may be desirable to reexamine the view that intervention is not an appropriate substitute for appropriate interest-rate policy. Larger intervention could mitigate the extent to which interest-rate fluctuations are translated into exchange-rate fluctuations.

The question would arise, nevertheless, whether greater concern should attach to the movement of the spot rate or the forward rate. When the interest differential changes, the forward discount or premium must also change, if interest parity is to be preserved, as it usually is. A constant spot rate in the face of a rising U.S. interest rate and interest-rate differential would imply a depreciation of the forward dollar. That certainly would not reflect the fundamentals of the situation. Some rise in the spot rate would, therefore, seem appropriate when the interest differential increases, enough perhaps to make a decline in the forward rate unnecessary or even to allow for some increase in the forward rate, but less than would have occurred without intervention.

In any event, the volume of short-term funds in the market that can move in response to interest-rate differentials is very large. The volume of intervention that would be required to offset the impact of such interest-rate arbitrage on exchange rates would also have to be very large. Clearly,. therefore, there are fairly narrow limits to such a policy even if it were decided to employ intervention to offset the exchange-rate effects of interest-rate arbitrage.

Reserve Considerations

Intervention policy is influenced by considerations of foreign-exchange reserve policy in various ways. One way is a country's policy about the level of its foreign-exchange reserves. When a weak currency is supported by its home authorities, these authorities lose reserves. When it is supported by the authorities of a strong currency, those authorities gain reserves. Either may be welcome or unwelcome to the respective authorities. Typically, monetary authorities are more concerned about excessive reduction in their reserves than excessive accumulation. Their willingness to intervene will be affected accordingly.

Technically, however, it is quite possible to overcome these effects, provided there is a way of harmonizing the interests of the two authorities. If, for instance, both authorities want to avoid reserve losses and perhaps accumulate reserves, the bulk of the intervention activity could be shifted to the authority of the strong currency and away from that of the weak currency. Alternatively, the two central banks could trade to each other the currencies acquired in the intervention, thereby restoring their respective losses and increases in their reserves. This will not work, of course, if the central bank of the strong currency wants to avoid further reserve accumulation while the central bank of the weak currency wants to avoid further losses.

When floating became generalized, there was some belief that the need for exchange reserves would diminish, if not totally disappear. That has proved erroneous. Countries do desire reserves, often in amounts that imply that they contemplate having to intervene on a large scale. This attitude seems to prevail despite the fact that today it is relatively easy, for most countries, to increase or replenish their gross reserves by international borrowing.

The United States entered the floating period with a minimum of reserves. Gold reserves had ceased to be usable, and the only reserves that the United States owned were its reserve tranche in the International Monetary Fund and some SDR. For intervention operations, the United States had to rely on the Federal Reserve's swap network, that is, on the borrowing of reserves. Part of the move to more forceful defense of the dollar on 1 November 1978 was the acquisition of reserves through Carter notes, with the possibility of the additional issues. The United States became a foreign-exchange reserve-holding country, but on a scale incomparably smaller, in relation to its economy and its foreign trade, than other countries.

Reserves can be accumulated, of course, through purchase in the exchange market. That, however, would have an effect on the exchange rate of the dollar. Given the intervention principle of not driving the rate, accumulation of reserves in a falling dollar market would be precluded in any event. Accumulation in a rising market would be possible.

Perhaps because it has never been a large reserve-holding country, public opinion in the United States seems to be particularly sensitive to the risks inherent in reserve holding. Under a floating system, the value of foreign-exchange reserves is bound to fluctuate. This may mean losses for the reserve-holding authorities. Indeed, the central banks with the strongest currencies have had very sizable losses on their dollar holdings, only partly compensated by the higher dollar interest rate in the most recent years. If the United States were to acquire large reserves, and perhaps suffer losses on them, there would probably be concern that the taxpayers' money was being wasted.

The reserve policy of the United States, except for the decision to issue Carter bonds, has been largely a passive one. No positive decisions to accumulate reserves, or to avoid accumulation, have been made. The experience and policies of the other countries suggest that a major country not practicing benign or any other type of neglect of currency does indeed need reserves. The United States no longer occupies a position in which it can claim to be exempt from such considerations. In the course of time, therefore, the United States may well decide to accumulate reserves. It would be better if such a development occurred as a result of well-thought-out policies rather than of the accidents of the market.

A Quantitative Approach to Intervention?

The possibility of losses on exchange reserves requires monetary authorities to give thought to the aspect of risk. Risk is not minimized by the absence of reserves. If a country relies on borrowings of foreign exchange—through swaps, for example—or through medium-term notes as the United States has done, it also incurs a risk, since it is indebted in foreign currencies. Risk is minimized only by avoiding any long or short position in foreign exchange. This would be equivalent to foregoing the possibility of market intervention.

Risk, however, must be meaningfully defined. It is not meaningful to focus only on exchange-rate gains and losses without taking into account related interest-rate effects. Typically, the stronger a currency, the lower its interest rates and vice versa. Hence, a central bank that has losses on a weak currency that it holds is likely to find itself compensated, in some degree, by interest earnings that are higher than would be the earnings on alternative assets in its own currency. Precise accounting would be difficult. But to ignore totally the interest-rate aspect, as seems to be the predominant practice among central banks nowadays, conveys a false impression of gains and losses and of the risks encountered in holding foreign currencies. If interest-rate differentials exactly match exchange-rate movements, of course, there would be no net gains and losses at all.

Monetary authorities also have to look at the risk factor of intervention in a more short-run sense. When intervention takes place during a period of pronounced exchange-rate movements in one particular direction, a time will come when the rate may be thought of as particularly high or particularly low. Central banks will be increasingly willing to support their currency because they believe they are buying it at a low price. If the rate then reverses, but is still high, they may be much less willing to support the currency that previously had been strong and is beginning to decline because they see themselves buying it at a high price. These perceptions of risk may, of course, prove erroneous if the central banks' judgment of the future of a currency is no better than that of the market. Nevertheless, they will influence intervention policies. Cooperation and consultation among central banks is particularly important at such points to avoid brusque shifts in intervention activity that might lead to market disorder.

For most countries, intervention means intervention in the market for the dollar and the local currency. That follows from the reserve-currency role of the dollar. An important exception is the operation of the European Monetary System (EMS), in which operations occur between currencies at opposite ends of the 4.5 percent band within which the EMS currencies are allowed to move.

For the United States, on the other hand, there is no obvious counterpart to the dollar in which to intervene. The DM has been by far the most important intervention currency for the United States, reflecting the importance of the Federal Republic of Germany in international trade and finance as well as the openness of the German economy to all kinds of international transactions. Nevertheless, the DM is only one of several potential currencies in which the Federal Reserve could intervene and indeed has in the past intervened.

Moreover, it is not entirely clear that concentration on any single currency is desirable. There is a tendency for market interest to focus on the currencies that are strongest at the moment. They are the principal objective of international investors. Accordingly, it is the strong currencies, and principally the DM, that become natural counterparts for U.S. intervention policy. The consequence is, however, that U.S. intervention tends to focus interest on the strongest currencies. In that way, it may contribute to unfavorable comparisons to which the dollar may be exposed by that relationship, at least in appearance. It would seem to be in the interest of the United States to counteract this tendency and to broaden the range of currencies in which it intervenes. That would reduce the unfavorable comparison of exchange-rate performances by shifting attention to some less-strong currencies. It would also provide a broader basis for intervention since, after all, the market for any one currency does not reflect the totality of flows in the U.S. balance of payments.

Since the Federal Reserve has swap arrangements with fourteen countries and the Bank for International Settlements totaling $30 billion, there is clearly a possibility of broadening the range of intervention. In the case of some countries this may not be possible because of the market limitations, or because the other currency would not be strong enough. But, in an emerging multi-reserve currency system, it is become increasingly anachronistic to focus U.S. intervention policy almost exclusively on the DM.

Most intervention is price-oriented, that is, it seeks to influence the exchange rate in a specific way, although not necessarily to achieve a particular level. The amount of intervention is allowed to depend on circumstances. An alternate procedure would be to make decisions concerning the amount of intervention, leaving the price effect to be determined by the market. There is an evident parallel here between exchange-market operations and domestic open-market operations. Both can be designed to influence either price or quantity.

Federal Reserve open-market operations have moved all the way from pure price orientation to almost pure quantity orientation. In its early days, during the 1950s, the Federal Reserve open-market policy was guided by "the tone and feel of the market." That meant to influence short-term interest rates in a direction that would tend to stabilize the economy. It was quantitatively imprecise and left a great deal to ad hoc judgment, particularly of the manager of the open-market account. From that condition, Federal Reserve open-market policy has moved increasingly in a quantity-oriented direction. Beginning in 1970, money-supply targets were established, but considerable importance still attached to interest rates. Beginning in 1979, money-supply targets were implemented in a more rigorous manner, allowing interest rates to fluctuate more widely. In addition to improving the chances of attaining money-supply targets, it keeps the Federal Operations Market Committee (FOMC) in closer touch with the operations of the open-market desk.

In the exchange-market intervention field, we are still in the condition of the 1950s, guiding ourselves by "tone and feel of the market." When intervention takes place, it is because the rate has moved and a need is perceived to prevent disorder. There is no way of knowing what the amount of intervention will eventually add up to. If the pressure ends the next day, there will be no more intervention. If it continues, intervention may run into the billions. Countries like Germany and Japan, operating on similar principles, have on occasion found themselves spending well over $10 billion on support of their currencies during a relatively short period of time. In 1977, the central banks of the world spent $35 billion net on support of the dollar. There is, in other words, no quantitative control over the volume of intervention. This is a very broad way of interpreting the concept of countering disorder in the exchange markets.

An intervention policy that would decide the scale of intervention but leave the setting of the exchange rate to the market would have two principal advantages. First, it would implement more fully the principle underlying the floating rate system: that exchange rates are to be determined by fundamental market factors. The present approach retains a good deal of judgment as to the appropriate rate, even though it does not pretend to fix any rate. If experience in the domestic monetary-policy field is any guide, the authorities tended to be reluctant to admit the need for substantial rate changes and to be too slow in yielding to market pressures for their implementation. That, of course, had been the experience also under the old fixed exchange-rate system. The technique focusing on the quantity of intervention rather than the rate would have a better chance of producing equilibrium exchange rates.

Second, a quantity-oriented approach would help control the present open-ended character of much intervention. It would enable the authorities to plan more effectively, instead of leaving action to be determined chiefly by the course of events.

The present system leaves open whether a given intervention on a given day will be an isolated event or the beginning of a multi-billion-dollar operation. Leaning against the wind can cumulate to very large amounts if the wind keeps blowing. This makes planning for future availability of resources and for future market operations more difficult. At an extreme, it would lead to conditions of reserve exhaustion that had not been foreseen or prepared for, or to very large accumulations with possibly inflationary consequences.

A quantity-oriented intervention approach would not lend itself to all types of situations. There may be unforeseen shocks to the market that do not allow for judgments as to optimal quantity of intervention and call for a rate-oriented approach. There may be other situations in which it is difficult to formulate a basis for a quantity-oriented approach. The quantity-oriented approach seems promising principally in two cases.

1. When there is a need to accumulate a given volume of foreign exchange over a particular time, such as for the purpose of repaying indebtedness. This could be the case of the Federal Reserve System when it has drawn on its swaps, or of the Treasury when it has used resources derived from the Carter notes.

2. When projections can be made of future flows in the balance of payments. Current-account deficits and surpluses are the most obvious example. Such projections are made routinely by national and international agencies. Given such a projection, a decision could be made to finance some part, if not the whole of it, by feeding exchange into the market in case of a deficit and by drawing it out of the market in the case of a surplus. This would still leave to the flows of the market the task of determining the exchange rate. All that intervention would do would be to change somewhat the balance between supply and demand. If the market strongly believes that the rate should move to some particular level, its forces will prevail over those of intervention. But, if the market is merely trying to estimate what the balance of supply and demand will be, the supply or demand emanating from intervention will have its weight. That is essentially what is happening to interest rates in the domestic arena under the Federal Reserve's new money-supply procedures. It would probably be effective also in the exchange market under a quantity-oriented approach.

Discussion

Question: Is it not possible that exchange-rate volatility might be much greater if central banks follow your suggestion and pursue an international reserve target and allow the market to determine the exchange rate freely?

Answer: It is true than when you control more firmly one thing, either quantity or price, the other thing will be less stable. Since we now try to control more firmly the quantity of money, its price or interest rate has been less stable. In the same sense, I think if we were to try to influence—I would not say control—the flow of foreign exchange in the market by intervention, then it may well happen that exchange rates would move more, but they might move better than they would move otherwise. Furthermore, so long as the authorities try to influence the price, that is, the exchange rate, the chances of error are always present, and the temptation to prevent a sufficiently rapid adjustment or adjustment in the right direction is always there.

Question: Why have there been such large fluctuations in exchange rates during the 1970s, even though central banks have tried to stabilize the rates?

Answer: If the market at a given time thinks that the rate of a given currency should go down by x percent, and it has a firm price expectation about that, then there is no way in which intervention can prevent the market from going there. Take an example. Under the old Bretton Woods system, a cyclical disequilibrium did not justify a devaluation of a currency. Only a fundamental disequilibrium did. Nevertheless, we have seen that cyclical current-account deficits and surpluses such as we have had under floating now do affect exchange rates. In other words, the market seems to disagree with the formulators of the Bretton Woods system, and it seems to think that cyclical current-account deficits and surpluses should lead to rate changes.

One might be of a different opinion. One might say that the market does not look far enough, and if the market did look far enough it would not change the rate. One cannot be sure of this, but the pattern has been so striking with current-account imbalances causing large exchange-rate movements that one wonders if this is not a serious deficit in the present system.

Question: A central bank cannot avoid having a domestic monetary policy, since it has to supply base money, and in doing so it can emphasize the supply side or it can emphasize the price side. But the central bank does not have to have an exchange-rate policy or a reserve policy. If the belief is firmly held that the market can do it better, why have exchange-rate or reserve policies?

Answer: Yes, that is very logical. I think the market is usually more right than the authorities, but not always. Whether it is right to try to moderate the movement of a rate does not depend in some degree on whether one thinks the market is exactly right. When you begin to suspect that the market goes too far in making cyclical adjustments to imbalances that will be reversed, then you have a pretty important case in which the market is not right.

Part III
LDC Financing

8 LDC Financing: The Brazilian Perspective

Angelo Calmon De Sa

Brazil has become the biggest borrower in an international market trying to cope with the problems that were created by the two oil shocks. I would say that we have a different position in regard to the two oil shocks. On the first one, as I think we all know, Brazil decided to follow a policy not to restrain the growth of the country. To the contrary, we decided that we should invest a lot and we should borrow a lot to invest huge amounts of money in basic products.

We found in 1974, when we had a huge trade deficit of $4.7 billion, that oil was responsible for $2 billion of that deficit, meaning the increase that we had on our oil bills from 1973 to 1974. But the $2.7 billion additional that we had on our deficit was due to basic imports and capital-goods imports.

Brazil took this attitude of keeping the country growing, which we did for five years at an average rate of growth of 7 percent. We were able to put the country back in a trade balance account again by 1977 because of a lot of import substitution and because oil prices had not moved up from 1974 on up to 1978. So the positive result of our policy from 1974 to 1979 was the growth that the country experienced, the structure we have built up that makes us better able to face the second oil shock, as will be shown by the figures that follow.

An example of one basic sector where Brazil has invested heavily and has changed completely from a previous dependence is the steel industry. In 1974 Brazil was importing about 5 million tons of steel up to a value of $1.5 billion. By 1978, we were already having a surplus on our steel trade of about $180 million, and Brazil has not stopped increasing consumption on steel. This is due to the fact that we have tremendously increased our output on steel production, as we did in many other basic products like petrochemicals, chemical products, paper and pulp, and also in the capital-goods area.

The negative aspect of this policy—as everyone is well aware —was that the increase in our indebtedness was very sharp, and the rate of inflation increased as well. As we were investing a lot in quite long-term maturity product, a great deal of stress was placed on the structure of supply of goods and services in the country, and, therefore, the demand was far above the supply; that is one of the main reasons why inflation has gone up in Brazil besides, of course, the oil price increases.

But we had had an additional complication at the end of this period that made it even more difficult to cope with the second oil shock. A major political evolution was occurring in our country. Between 1975 and 1979 the government started to move in the direction of a full democracy. First, freedom of the press and more political freedom were allowed, and in January 1979 all the special powers reserved to the Executive Branch were removed from the Constitution. As a result of these changes Brazil is quite a different society from what it had been in fifteen years before 1979.

The social pressures became greater and, of course, wage increases started to exceed inflation levels. When the second oil shock arrived inflation was already accelerating rapidly. As is well known, in nominal value the increase in oil prices during the second oil shock was much bigger than during the first one. We had an $8 increase on the price of a barrel from 1973 to 1974, and from the end of 1978 until the end of 1980 we had a $20 per barrel increase in the price of oil. It is not difficult to imagine how difficult it has been for Brazil to face this fact.

However, even with an increased oil bill of about $6.5 billion from 1978 to 1980, our performance has been relatively good, mainly due to the fact that the structure of the Brazilian economy is in much better shape today than it was previously. We are dependent, of course, on imported oil, but we are far less dependent on imports of other basic products. We should be ending this year with a trade deficit between $2.5 billion and $3 billion. That will be smaller than the increase we had in the oil bill from 1978 on. If not for the second oil shock, therefore, Brazil would be running a sizable trade surplus on its account.

This shows that the strategy Brazil adopted after the first oil shock, when there was room to maneuver—the indebtedness of Brazil at the beginning of that period was relatively small—was good, but we know that from now on it is quite a different story. Brazil can not go on borrowing more and more. This has already been noticed by the Brazilian government, and it can be seen from the following figures that the tendency is to reduce the rate of growth of our indebtedness.

By 1978 indebtedness had increased from $32 billion to about $44 billion at the end of the year. That is an almost 40 percent increase in indebtedness in one year. In 1979 the figure rose $44 billion to $50 billion, or a bit less than a 15 percent increase in indebtedness. In 1980 Brazil's indebtedness reached $55 billion, or 10 percent above the figure of December 1979.

It is important to maintain this trend. The fact that exports have moved exactly in the opposite direction of indebtedness is a very positive development. The rate of growth in exports has increased, especially from 1978 on. In 1978 exports were $12.6 billion, roughly 5 percent above the level of exports in 1977. In 1979 they rose to $15.4 billion, meaning an almost 25 percent increase. By 1979, then, Brazil already had a higher rate of growth on export earnings than on indebtedness. The figures for 1980 are around $20 billion of exports, or about a 30 percent increase on export earnings.

Taking into account the fact that 1978, 1979, and 1980 were all poor agricultural years, then the increase in export earning came mainly from the increased exports of manufactured goods. The question then arises: Will not Brazil be affected by the current worldwide recession? I think not, for two reasons. First, exports to new markets, like the Middle East, Nigeria, and other countries in Latin America that are not under recession are greatly increasing. Second, Brazil's share of the market in industrialized products is still very small, so it remains unaffected. Brazil can continue as its done to grow on its exports of industrialized products.

Brazil today is faced with the fact, as all bankers know, that there is some concern about its situation in the international market; there is concern that Brazil will face problems in coping with financial needs next year. If the government continues the current very restrictive monetary and government-expenditures policies, it should be able—slowing the rate of growth of the country for next year—to cope with its financial needs because of the big shift on its trade accounts following the reduction in rate of growth.

It is clear that some internal adjustments of the economy are needed. The government, however, has changed priorities; emphasis will now be placed on the energy sector, the energy-substitution program, and the agricultural sector. If production is increased in the latter, two problems can be solved at the same time: helping to reduce inflation by a bigger supply of food and helping our balance of trade if we have a bigger surplus on our production of agricultural products. Also, of course, the government is putting a lot of emphasis on helping export-oriented industries.

These are the priorities that the government has today, and it is interesting to note that in the energy area—a major factor in the imbalance of Brazil's foreign accounts—internal production of oil is being developed; it is expected that production will reach a level of about 500,000 barrels per day by 1985 from the fields already discovered.

The alcohol program, started about three years ago, produced only 500 million liters of alcohol in its first year; this year it will produce 4 billion liters of alcohol, and by 1985 about 11 billion liters of alcohol should be produced, the equivalent of 180,000 barrels per day.

Fuel-oil substitution is being implemented in the cement industry (the main consumer of fuel), and this should help save an additional 120,000-130,000 barrels per day by 1985.

If that happens, oil imports will be reduced by 1985 to about 700,000 barrels per day; today, about 900,000 barrels per day are imported.

Brazil has another major advantage in energy production that few other countries possess. It is not widely known that Brazil does not use oil to generate electricity. All its electricity comes from hydroelectric power, and there is the potential to develop hydroelectric power as an even more important source of energy. Today oil accounts for 40 percent of total Brazilian energy production and hydro accounts for 32 percent, but this should change dramatically within four or five years as becomes more and more important. With the completion of two major projects, hyrdoelectric will assume a more important role as a source of energy in Brazil. The problem of inflation remains but it is hoped that the course of action taken by the government will be able to cope with this problem and solve it.

In the social area, there has been in the last few months a very encouraging reaction from the unions. A year ago, in 1979, they were making claims on wage increases that were quite unbearable for the companies involved and were no doubt a source of inflation, but recently wage agreements were settled quite reasonably. By and large, they have been quite responsible.

A certain amount of unemployment has started to occur in Brazil. Unemployment in Brazil is quite different from unemployment in the United States. Brazil has no system to support the unemployed; consequently, unemployment there causes severe hardship.

In light of the recent moderate behavior of the unions, it is not thought that the government will face a major problem in reducing the rate of growth of the country. This is the policy Brazil should follow, and if it does so I do not foresee any major problem for Brazil to continue to finance its current-account deficits in the coming years.

9 Venezuelan Investments in LDC Development

Roberto Guarnieri

The sudden and significant change in Venezuela economic and financial situation brought about by the oil price increase did not take the authorities by surprise in terms of policy response. This matter had been to a large extent anticipated by the government, and in light of its possible distorting effects it had become clear that there must be a thoroughly *managed* adjustment process. It was felt that the markets, if left by themselves as they had been in past situations, would tend to produce a kind of adjustment that might be contrary to the social and economic goals of the authorities in terms of price stability, balanced growth, and adequate attention to collective needs.

Furthermore, what one might call the international requirements of such a policy, that is, the need to take into account, in a meaningful way, the question of global balance-of-payments financing and adjustment and, in general, the issue of recycling were duly incorporated in the policy reaction of the authorities.

The Venezuelan economic-policy conceptual framework of 1974, which still rules in the present circumstances, could be appreciated in terms of a simple set of goals and requirements comprising, or related to, the following basic propositions: (1) maintenance of internal price stability; (2) efficient capital-resource allocation; and (3) effective contribution to international balance-of-payments financing and adjustment. In this context it was thought that the implementation of the required policies in the light of the new—much larger—dimensions of economic and financial flows and stocks could not be efficiently handled within the existing institutional framework.

To give just a broad idea of what was involved in terms of changes in key variables, suffice it to say that the country's total exports at current prices increased from 3.2 billion dollars in 1972 to 11 billion in 1974. Central Government ordinary revenues similarly increased from 3.3 billion dollars in 1972 to 10.6 billion in 1974, while GDP, also at current prices, went from 14.1 billion dollars in 1972 to 26.5 billion in 1974.

It was then decided to set up the Venezuelan Investment Fund (VIF), which was to be a tailor-made organization that would deal directly in the activities related to the three previously enumerated policy goals. According to its statutes, the fund was to engage in direct lending and equity participation in domestic projects for the development of so-called basic sectors.

Broadly speaking, this included the exploitation and processing of natural resources, including hydroelectric generation but excluding the petroleum sector, and also shipbuilding, shipping, and transportation. In practice, through global loans to specialized credit institutions for on-lending, the fund has also become involved in the financing of projects in the manufacturing and the agricultural sector.

Second, the fund was to be henceforth the institution to design and implement the government economic cooperation programs with other LDCs and with multilateral aid and development finance institutions such as the World Bank, the Interamerican Development Bank, the Caribbean Development Bank, the Central American Bank for Economic Integration, the Andean Development Corporation, the International Fund for Agricultural Development, and the OPEC Special Fund.

Third, in acknowledgment of the initial relative abundance of capital resources in terms of available development projects, the area of finance management proper was strongly emphasized to insure the adequate temporary financial investment of funds. It is worth mentioning in this regard that the Venezuelan Fund is not allowed to place any money in the domestic monetary and capital market. It all has to be invested abroad.

It could be said, therefore, that not only directly—through the external cooperation programs—but also indirectly—by the placing of available funds within the international financial system—the Venezuelan contribution to international balance-of-payments financing and adjustment and to the recycling process in general after 1974 has been very significant. The extent of this contribution is shown by the fund's consolidated balance sheet of December 1975.

Total assets	$5.2 billion
Financial—short- and medium-term investments	$4.0 billion
External cooperation	$0.8 billion
Investment in local development projects and other items	$0.4 billion

It is worth mentioning that the main item of the external cooperation account was a 500 million dollar 15-year loan, granted by the VIF to the World Bank in August 1974. It was the first instance of substantial direct lending by an OPEC member to an international-development institution, and, as an interesting feature, it may be noted that the loan was partly denominated in U.S. dollars and partly in Venezuelan currency.

It is fair to say that not only did the Venezuelan authorities act immediately in the area of direct recycling, but they were among the first to recognize the special nature and requirements of the payments imbalances arising from the oil price increases, and to behave accordingly.

To be consistent with the view that was then being expressed by Venezuelan representatives in different organizations—particularly in the IMF—regarding the appropriate conditionality and terms to be applied to the financing of countries with balance-of-payments deficits due to their oil-import bill increase and together with the decision to participate actively in the funding of the IMF oil facilities then being set up under Johannes Witteveen's leadership, the authorities realized the need to provide direct assistance to most affected neighboring LDs. This aid would not only cover the additional cost of oil imports but would also help them in the financing of national key development projects.

In December 1974 at a meeting of heads of states of two Central American countries, Panama and Venezuela, the so-called Caracas facility was agreed upon. It provided for the automatic financing of the oil-import bills of such countries, in excess of a floor value calculated on a price basis of six dollars per barrel. The scheme started with the financing of 100 percent of the calculated additional cost in the first year of operation (1975). This was then to be scaled down by a 16.6 percent factor in each successive year, so that the facility would expire in 1980.

The financing was to be in the form of Venezuelan Investment Fund quarterly, six-year term deposits in the central banks of the beneficiaries. The key feature of the agreement was that such deposits could later be converted into long-term loans whenever it could be shown that the local-currency equivalent would be applied to the financing of development projects already approved and carrying a loan from an international development institution such as the World Bank or the Interamerican Development Bank. The interest on the Venezuelan loan was to be equal to that of the principal.

Total commitments under this scheme, whose benefits were later also extended to Jamaica and the Dominican Republic, that are already almost fully disbursed and converted into long-term loans amount to about 700 million dollars. This sum is, however, less than one-third of total aid and finance provided by Venezuela since 1974 (mostly by the VIF, but also by other institutions such as the Export Financing Fund and the Central Bank) to other LDCs either bilaterally or through direct financing or the setting up of trust funds in regional- and international-development institutions.

Before proceeding with the consideration of immediate future prospects, it can be stated that as of the end of September 1980, total commitments, of the VIF only, amounted to about 2.3 billion dollars, of which 1.9 billion had already been paid out.

Let us now look at Venezuela's immediate plans in the area of international-development finance. Before doing so, however, it is necessary to consider at least two relevant issues that have become increasingly important over the years and that have to be taken into account for their direct bearing on the scope of the authorities to pursue and strengthen these programs of international economic cooperation and balance-of-payments assistance.

First, government resource allocation, after the large increases in oil revenues in 1974 and the following year, has not been fully consistent with a balanced attention by the public sector to immediate collective needs, as against the provision for future private needs through public capital investments in the productive sectors. It is now clear that relatively little regard was paid to improve the capacity to supply basic services and to develop other projects directly related to the standard of living and the quality of life of the population, particularly of the lower-income groups, such as low-cost housing and public-recreation facilities.

The emphasis until very recently was on heavy industrial development. The insufficient application of government resources to expand the capacity to meet demand for public goods and basic services has aggravated an already difficult situation of income distribution. This has been worsened further by illegal immigration from neighboring countries, estimated at about 2.5 million people over a total registered population of 14 million.

The present relative inadequacy of the health system, public transportation, water and electricity supply, and basic education, has become fully apparent. To correct this situation is one of the stated priorities of the present administration. This is certainly consistent with a more equitable and just society and, in light of the very substantial nominal national-income increase that has occurred over the last six years, absolutely warranted politically.

It can be argued, moreover, that the present imbalance in the cumulative allocation of public funds is not only socially undesirable but also questionable from the strictly economic point of view. In the past, the main constraint to faster development has been the lack of an adequate labor force, not only of the specialized kind but also of manpower amenable to basic on-the-job training. There is certainly an urgent need to implement programs to improve health, educational, and nutritional standards in the country, as well as to strengthen fundamental social institutions through appropriate government promotion.

The degree of general awareness of this deficiency is, as has been discussed, extremely *high*. So is the determination of the government to overcome it. But, as will be easily realized, the financial requirements of such a socially oriented economic policy are very large. This is of course quite apparent to all and, therefore, it is not as politically feasible as it was a few years ago to divert limited resources, no matter what the purpose, away from this most urgent domestic task.

There is also the burden of an increasing public debt. As of the end of 1979, outstanding registered external debt amounted to 8.2 billion dollars or 17 percent of 1979 GDP. The corresponding figures for December 1973 were only 1.2 billion and 7 percent of GDP.

It is in a sense a kind of double paradox—or so it is perceived by public opinion—that the use of external savings by the Venezuelan economy has accelerated during this period of substantially increased foreign-exchange receipts. It is also noted that the country has been borrowing heavily, at high cost, while, at the same time, lending long term to other countries and international organizations. It should be noted that much of the debt has been contracted to maintain operational certain autonomous institutions and public-sector enterprises in light of inadequate management, including inefficient financial planning, and a prevailing situation of below marginal cost-pricing and tariffing.

No doubt this could all be rationalized to the desired extent, but the fact is that the question of the public external debt has become a sensitive economic and political issue; this was not the case two or three years ago. This is a situation of unquestionable relevance, of course, for the formulation of a future program of Venezuelan financial investments in the LDCs, particularly when about 21 pecent of total 1981 budgeted expenditure will be for external debt servicing.

These questions have been considered in some detail because their relevance needs to be appreciated in order to assess the full importance of the new Venezuelan program of economic cooperation with Central American and Caribbean countries that is presently in the process of being signed by the parties concerned. In accordance with the original principle held by the authorities that the oil-induced payments imbalances are of structural nature and therefore require, among other things, long-term resources to promote the necessary internal adjustment, the new Venezuelan cooperation program, which Mexico has joined, will provide for foreign exchange financing convertible into long-term loans. It is, in a sense, the continuation of the Caracas facility of 1974.

Since Mexico has now become a major oil exporter, it has been agreed that the supply of oil to the beneficiaries of the agreement shall be on a fifty-fifty basis by Venezuela and Mexico. This relationship is not only to apply in the aggregate, but also for each and every one of the countries that are party to the agreement. These countries are: Barbados, Costa Rica, the Dominican Republic, El Salvador, Guatamala, Honduras, Jamaica, Nicaragua, and Panama. This agreement covers one year of oil imports. The mechanism is similar to the one applied since 1974. Each supplying country will finance up to 30 percent of the total cost of the oil by means of deposits in the central banks of the countries concerned. These deposits are to be gradually converted into long-term loans.

It may be worthwhile to briefly explain the detailed procedure involved in the case of Venezuela. The Venezuelan Ministry of Energy and Mines will establish for each beneficiary the maximum oil-import volume allowed under the agreement for the twelve-month period beginning in August 1980. The Venezuelan Investment Fund will then proceed to make quarterly deposits in the central banks of the recipient countries for an amount equal to 30 percent of the total estimated oil-import bill of the following quarter. In fact, the first deposits now in the process of being made will actually cover to the end of this year. Fifty percent of the deposits will be denominated in U.S. dollars, the other 50 percent in Venezuelan bolivars.

Any adjustments arising from differences between estimated and actual oil-import values will be made in the following quarter. The deposits are to have a 5-year term and will carry a 4 percent annual interest rate. The recipient countries will then be allowed to submit requests to the Venezuelan Investment Fund for the conversion of such deposits into loans of up to twenty years maturity for the financing of development institutions, as was the case for the 1974 facility.

The projects that will be eligible for these loans are to be related to the following areas: (1) domestic energy resources; (2) natural resources in general; (3) the export sectors. Special consideration will also be given to projects or programs that are instrumental to the process of regional economic integration and to the development of trade between the beneficiaries of such loans and Venezuela. Total financing to be provided by Venezuela under this scheme for the period August 1980 to July 1981 has been estimated at above 300 million dollars, on the basis of a constant average oil price of $35 per barrel over the period concerned.

One might point out, perhaps, that in the present circumstances of the international oil market it is not unlikely that the actual price be above the one used for these estimates. That amount of aid is then to be considered a floor to the flow of concessional finance to be provided by Venezuela to these LDCs over such period of time. It is also important to stress the highly concessional nature of this program.

Some might say that the fact that the agreement only covers a twelve-month period reflects the view that this matter requires frequent assessment and evaluation. This does not necessarily imply, of course, any decision on the part of Venezuela to eventually discontinue a meaningful participation in balance-of-payments and development financing of LDCs.

This new Venezuelan external-aid program is a significant contribution by a high-absorbing reduced size, oil-exporting country, itself facing some very difficult choices and constraints at home to the international financial adjustment in the year to come. It is, furthermore, another instance of Venezuela's preoccupation with the requirements of a stable world economy.

It should also be stressed that in spite of its high degree of concession-ality, the financing to be provided is in no way tied to purchases of Venezuelan goods and services.

In designing and approving this economic cooperation program, the Venezuelan authorities are firmly convinced that the overcoming of the pres-ent, very difficult prospects for the world economy requires the joint effort of all members of the international community, given a realistic reciprocal acknowledgment of the relative position, weight, and influence of each. Good judgment, initiative, and determination are certainly required on all fronts, including the national level and in the international-development and monetary institutions. The role of the IMF cannot, I believe, be overstressed, as Johannes Witteveen suggests in chapter 3 of this book; it will be crucial. Not only will it provide the necessary short and medium-term balance-of-payments financing as required but also, one hopes, it will provide the kind of leadership necessary in the present difficult cir-cumstances to prevent the adoption of national economic policies inconsis-tent with a free and growing world economy. Within this context, the work and the initiative of the Group of Thirty and the Global Interdependence Center is to be commended. I hope that meetings such as this conference will truly help in shaping a collectively adequate attitude toward meeting the challenges of the years to come.

10 Structural Adjustments in Developing Countries

Robert Slighton

The subject of this chapter is the direct and indirect effects of oil prices on the economic performance of oil-importing developing countries. There are various ways this question can be addressed. The journalist's question is: Will recycling work for the developing countries this time around? Frankly, that question must be translated in order to answer it. The central banker's question is: Will interruptions of debt service by the developing countries create significant problems for the liquidity of the international banking system? The economist's question is somewhat different. His basic question is whether the supply of international lending, considered together with the willingness of the developing countries to take appropriate policy measures, will be sufficient to permit an orderly adjustment to the less-favorable international economic environment, or whether this adjustment will tend to be delayed and hence more severe.

Given the number of times the word adjustment appears in this discussion, I should add that adjustment in this sense refers to growth: Will growth be reduced moderately or will it be reduced significantly? Will growth paths be relatively stable or will they be unstable?

Given the extreme diversity of the countries under discussion, it is obvious that no simple answer to the general question is possible. The difficulties are further confounded by the increasing uncertainty as to just how unfavorable the international environment is likely to be. Nonetheless, at least with respect to the broad outlines of a response—and I say response rather than answer—there is a reasonable degree of consensus.

In particular, even with highly favorable assumptions as to the future price of oil it is agreed that virtually all oil-importing developing countries will need to respond to the increased payments imbalances arising from the latest round of oil price increases more in terms of policy adjustment as opposed to continued borrowing than they did in 1974-1975.

In short, the ultimate effect of the second oil-price shock on the growth of the oil-importing developing economies will be somewhat more severe. Further, there is agreement that the willingness of the international financial community to lend to the oil-importing developing countries is relatively sensitive, but with a significant lag, to the willingness of the governments of these countries to take adjustment measures.

As a corollary to that proposition, it is agreed that the willingness of the developing nations to take adjustment measures is a greater source of uncertainty as to whether adjustment will be gradual or abrupt than is the supply of international lending.

What I have called this agreed response to our basic question is thus a doubly contingent answer. It is contingent first on what can be presumed about the price of oil, and it is also contingent on the rapidity of policy adjustment in the developing countries.

I will primarily discuss this second contingency. In particular, one aspect of the adjustment question, structural adjustment, the long-term changes in the structure of production and demand, will be examined. I choose this focus not out of any conviction that the other aspect of adjustment, changes in the current levels of demand for imports or current-demand management, is unimportant.

Indeed for a number of countries whose adjustment to the first oil-price shock was relatively incomplete, such policy changes are essential for maintenance of orderly borrowing relationships over the next few years. But this is well understood. What has received less attention is the extent to which the recent changes in the international economic environment have increased the costs in terms of growth foregone of a wide range of domestic policies commonly found in the developing countries that bias long-run resource allocation. What these policy biases are, why their costs in terms of foregone growth have increased, and what the likelihood is that they will operate with lessened force in the future are the next questions to be examined.

A quick review is in order of just what changes in the economic environment have taken place. What are the oil-importing developing countries adjusting to or failing to adjust to? Four structural changes arising directly or indirectly from the very large oil price increases are of particular importance. The first is so obvious as to be banal, that is, the very large increase in the relative international price of energy and goods that are energy-intensive in their production. Note that I stress the change in relative international prices. A key aspect of adjustment is the change of domestic prices in line with changes in international prices, and it is hardly news to a U.S. audience that this process is by no means automatic.

A second extremely important change is the increase in the difference between what the economist calls the scarcity price of foreign exchange and the exchange rate. The currencies of most oil-importing developing countries have typically been overvalued. The extent of this overvaluation has increased. The main factor behind this change is the reduced volume of nonenergy imports that can be financed by exports. This is in part the direct result of the higher relative price of oil and in part the result of lower growth in the industrialized countries, which implies both a lower growth of volume and somewhat lower relative price for developing-country exports.

Third, in most industries the productivity of capital has been reduced relative to the productivity of labor.

Fourth, the real cost of foreign borrowing has increased. This latter point is arguable, but I think it highly likely that the thrust of monetary policy in those countries that are the main international financial centers will work toward real interest rates over the next five years that are higher than those of the period of adjustment to the first oil-price shock.

The broad outlines of a policy strategy to promote efficient long-run adjustment to these structural changes flows more or less directly from the catalog of change itself. Such a policy strategy has three key elements.

First, the structure of domestic prices of energy and energy-intensive goods must be aligned with the structure of international prices. Second, the incentive to produce for export must be enhanced relative to the incentive to produce for the domestic market. Third, those elements of existing policy that bias choice of method of production in favor of capital-intensive technology should be eliminated.

The argument for the first of these policy shifts—the closer alignment of domestic and international prices of energy and energy-intensive goods—is obvious. Energy will not be conserved if it is not made more expensive. Domestic energy resources will not be developed if the price at which energy can be sold does not reflect its enhanced value. And most important of all in the short run, maintenance of domestic prices of energy and energy-intensive goods at levels persistently below international prices necessarily entails the provision of significant government subsidies that both reduce the level of domestic savings and accelerate the rate of money creation and inflation.

The argument for increased incentives to produce for export is equally straightforward. The relative social productivity of investment in export industries has been significantly increased, and the share of investment going to these industries must reflect that change. A variety of policy instruments can be brought to bear to insure such an adjustment. One is accelerated pace of devaluation of exchange rate. Another is favorable tariff or licensing treatment of imports of goods used in the production of exports.

Various of the policy measures needed to provide appropriate export incentives, particularly devaluation, are also important to the achievement of the third key adjustment objective, namely, encouraging less-capital-intensive methods of production.

The specific policy adjustment of greatest significance here, however, is the freeing of domestic capital markets from controls over interest rates and quantitative allocation of credit. Negative real-interest rates are both a powerful incentive for the employment of excessive amounts of capital and a powerful disincentive to save.

In this brief sketch of what policy changes are the key determinants of the efficiency of long-run adjustment, the word *must* have been used repeatedly. I have used this word because I accept the value judgments of the economists that policies promoting growth should be adopted. From the policymaker's point of view, however, the presumption of *must* hardly follows. Indeed the prescribed policy changes—my prescription for policy changes—involve going against the grain of three of the most deeply rooted policy biases common to the developing countries.

The first of these biases, and in some sense the root of the others, is distrust of the private-market system and the consequent tendency to allocate resources directly or indirectly by administrative decision. The second is the tendency to provide greater incentives for production for domestic markets than for export. The third is the tendency to bias the choice of method of production in favor of capital-intensive technologies.

In short, the economist's prescription for efficient structural adjustment is to do precisely what the policymaker has found most difficult or has been least willing to accomplish historically.

It would be a serious mistake to view these biases, these departures from economic efficiency, as capricious or arising out of some inability to perceive their consequences. The basic objective of the policymaker is maintenance of political legitimacy, not maximization of economic growth, and the acceptance of these biases has proved historically to be a relatively efficient way of maintaining legitimacy. In short, there is good reason to believe that policies promoting structural adjustment will be adopted considerably more slowly than the economist might hope.

A quick review of the progress to date in adjusting to the changed environment confirms this suspicion. With respect to the prescription of aligning the domestic and international prices of energy, the record of the oil-importing developing countries is decidedly mixed. In most countries the price of gasoline has been increased to levels promoting significant conservation, but the price of diesel fuel and kerosene, products viewed as having rather broader welfare implications, has typically lagged behind. The price of fertilizer is often heavily subsidized. And there are relatively few developing countries where the losses of state enterprises in the production of electricity are not a major drain on the capacity of the public sector to generate savings.

The response to date has been similarly tentative with respect to the prescription of increasing the incentive to export. Some countries, South Korea as an example, have devalued or accelerated the rate of mini-devaluation of their currencies. Others such as Brazil have announced their intention of gradually reversing recent losses in international competitiveness. Taken as a whole, however, exchange-rate movements, combined with changes in domestic prices, have been such that the competitive position of exporters in developing countries relative to producers in the industrialized nations is less favorable today than in the period immediately preceding the most recent round of oil price increases.

Even more discouraging is the response with respect to the prescription of reducing the bias in favor of capital-intensive methods of production and its corollary, the freeing of domestic-capital markets. In very few of the oil-importing developing countries are real interest rates positive. In some, Brazil in particular, real interest rates in the main domestic-capital markets have been massively negative, with the predictable consequence of rapid disintermediation from these markets and reduced private savings.

The conclusion is inescapable that relatively few developing countries have thus far shown signs of accepting the need to use the market mechanism to allocate credit and to change those policies chiefly responsible for the bias in favor of capital-intensive technology. Taiwan is perhaps an exception, and South Korea has taken tentative steps in this direction.

Where, then, do we stand? Given this description of the prospective willingness of the developing countries to take appropriate structural-adjustment measures, and given the existing institutional constraints on the supply of international lending, will adjustment be orderly or abrupt?

To put this question in another way, will the decline in the average growth of these economies over the next five years be moderate or severe? This brings our discussion back to the question we started with.

The answer depends critically on what is assumed about the future trend in the relative price of oil. Given the assumption of an upward trend in oil prices that does not significantly exceed the proposed OPEC long-run pricing strategy, there is good reason to be reasonably optimistic, particularly if we assume that the current constraints on lending by the multilateral organizations are relaxed somewhat.

Although the pace of policy adjustment in some countries is likely to prove insufficient to prevent a disruption of normal lending patterns, the great majority of developing countries now having reasonable access to long-term private credit markets would retain that access.

In short, most middle- and upper-income developing countries would be able both to service their foreign debt and to maintain growth rates significantly above those in the industrialized world.

Given a significantly less-optimistic view of the future course of oil prices—say an average annual increase in the relative price of oil between now and 1985 of 10 percent a year or so—these conclusions do not hold. Under that assumption, the maintenance of growth rates for the developing countries not markedly different from current levels implies a buildup of debt-service payments in most countries too large to be sustained over time, even if a significantly larger volume of nonconcessional lending were forthcoming from official or multilateral sources.

In mid-1980 this last assumption with respect to oil prices would probably have been judged pessimistic. As of November 1980 perceptions are rather different. The baseline projections of summer 1980 are now optimistic, and the pessimistic projections are more pessimistic. The reality of oil-price uncertainty has become more apparent.

What we must hope is that this increased awareness of the enormous uncertainty of the future price and availability of oil will result in a more rapid rate of adoption of policy measures promoting structural adjustment. Without this adjustment, the outlook for continued rapid growth in the oil-importing developing countries will be doubtful in all but the most optimistic oil-price scenarios.

Discussion

Comment 1: I agree fully with what Mr. Slighton has said. It is necessary to have adjustment in the developing countries. Futhermore, if we do so, then I do not see that we are going to have big problems with the recycling that is necessary.

Comment 2: There is another point worth making, namely, that the aggravating situation for LDCs is due, in part, to the recession in the developed countries. The LDC adjustment process has become much more difficult, since the world economy has been continually in a recession in recent years, and this provides very little stimulus for the exports of the developing countries. The LDCs could accomplish much more if the developed countries performed a little better on the growth score.

Question: I wonder whether it really would not be of interest to point out that it is not only the LDCs that must adjust. An adjustment policy must be carried out in the industrial countries, and this would show much greater results for the international monetary system than adjustment policies in developing countries.

Answer: I have to agree, but we were discussing the problem of recycling and financing the LDCs, and that is why I mentioned only adjustments in the LDCs. It is correct to say that all economies need to adjust to the higher oil prices, especially by allowing the internal prices of oil products to rise to world levels. We know that this has taken quite some time for the United States, and if the United States had adjusted the price five years ago, the picture would be quite different in regard to the oil situation all over the world.

Question: Will Brazil approach the IMF for debt rescheduling, and under what circumstances? Also, are Brazil's devaluation policies adequate in light of the domestic inflation rate?

Answer: It has already been announced by the minister of planning and also by the minister of finance that the cruzeiro devaluation will equal the Brazilian inflation rate minus the worldwide inflation rate. Next, with regard to borrowing from the IMF, it is not foreseen that Brazil will do this, because the Brazilian Congress and press as well as public opinion, all are very much against it. The major banks in the world that are very involved with Brazil are pressing for Brazil to go to the IMF in order to make it even clearer that Brazil will continue to follow the policy that has recently been adopted. However, I expect the inflation rate to fall and the trade account to improve significantly in the near future.

Question: Returning to the question of the adjustment that is necessary by industrial countries as well as the LDCs, would the panel not agree that if the recent wave of protectionism continues, then much of the efforts of the LDCs to improve their balance of payments is going to be frustrated? Would it not be true that adjustment on the part of the industrial countries should include a willingness to sacrifice old established mature industries whose products compete directly with the LDCs and to accelerate the switch to high-technology high-capital-intensive industries?

Answer 1: The threat of protectionism is a very real one, but in the United States try, more than in Europe, the political forces favoring freer trading are very strong. Hence, the question of whether or not protectionism will, in fact, be a major constraint on the ability of the developing countries to increase is still open. I am relatively optimistic about the situation in the United States, but less optimistic about Europe.

Answer 2: The question of protectionism is a serious one. The trade among LDCs is very small, so the prospect for these countries to maintain some adequate capacity to import is crucially dependent on their exports to the developed nations.

Answer 3: It is, in fact, very difficult bureaucratically to maintain an extremely strong protective barrier. Businessmen are considerbly more inventive than bureaucrats. When an import quota binds, then business goes to countries excluded from the quota, and it goes to industries that are technologically related, but not bureaucratically constrained. Thus, protectionism is something we can deplore, but it is not something that, in fact, will be a major source of difficulty.

Question: There seems to be a difference of opinion between two of the panelists. One panelist (panelist B) says that if energy prices are the right ones, if exchange rates are correct, and if interest rates are set properly, then perhaps the financing problem for LDCs is solved. In other words, all this is what the financial community is looking for; it makes little difference to the international banks what a developing country's inflation rate or trade deficit is as long as the policies are correct. On the other hand, another panelist (panelist A) appears to say that the most important factor from the point of view of the world financial community is to bring down the inflation rate and trade deficit. Is this a difference of perspective or of opinion?

Answer 2 (panelist A): If the right policy is adopted, then the improved inflation rate and trade deficit are going to happen in a country like Brazil as an outcome of the adjustment. And do not forget that Brazil is already following the correct policies.

Answer 2 (panelist B): I do not see a conflict either. I stressed the need to get the prices right; I am not seriously concerned about short-run austerity measures being taken. there is, however, more concern as to whether they are going to get the price right. If they do not get the prices right, then we will enter into a stop-go mode. Massive current-account imbalances will reappear as soon as the tight monetary and fiscal policies are dropped.

Question: I want to question the panel as to where capital formation as a policy fits into LDC finance. It is gaining increasing emphasis here in the United States. Is there a concept or a policy that deals with capital formation, and I am speaking of it in real terms, taking inflation into account?

Answer 1: This is a very relevant question, and I think the answer by and large is essentially negative. With the exception of a few countries, financial policies and interest-rate policies in most developing countries are not adjusted to the inflation rates that they are facing and, hence, we have so-called financial repression. A few countries have tried to avoid such a policy because it discourages saving and investment. South Korea and some countries in the southern tip of Latin America have tried for a number of years to follow realistic interest-rate policies, but they have had mixed results.

Answer 2: In the case of Brazil, we have established a system of indexing, and we have developed several types of instruments for getting the savings and for paying the real interest rate. This has helped a lot. More recently, however, we have started to constrain the level of the interest rate, and this has been very bad for capital formation.

Answer 3: Broadly speaking, the capital-formation problem in developing countries today is not that there is insufficient investment demand. Indeed, in many countries, the levels of investment last year or this year were somewhat excessive. The problem is the allocation of investment, and this is primarily a problem of not having relative prices correct. In addition, if there is a problem at the moment, it is with domestic saving. The short-run impact of the second oil-price shock has not been to depress the incentive to invest, but to depress the incentive to save. The immediate task, then, is to get savings rates up, particularly public saving rates. The other immediate task is to make sure that investment resources are being wisely used.

Part IV
Managing International
Reserves and Exchange
Rates

11 Exchange-Rate Regimes and the Quantity and Composition of International Reserves

Peter B. Kenen

This chapter is an attempt to sort out some of the connections between the reserve system and the exchange-rate system. As Robert Heller points out, these are too often treated as entirely separate dimensions of the international regime. There are two intimate connections between them that may be said to run in opposite directions. Those two connections can be segregated for orderly discussion by asking two questions. First, how has the move to floating exchange rates altered our views about the roles of reserves in the system—the need for reserves and the process of creating reserves? Second, how has the move to floating exchange rates altered our views about the roles of the various reserve assets—notably those of the dollar and the SDR in the International Monetary Fund?

Taking those questions in order, let us look first at the way that the exchange-rate regime has affected the need for reserves, then turn to the composition of reserves.

If, of course, we had a clean float, there would be no role for reserves in the monetary system, apart perhaps for a purely precautionary role, in that countries might want to hold reserves against the day when exchange rates were no longer to float freely.

Some countries might still want to accumulate financial claims on other countries, to earn interest and also to redistribute real consumption over time. Examples of this are the so-called low-absorbing OPEC countries, such as Saudi Arabia, which are piling up claims on the outside world and thus postponing the use of some of the income they earn from the sale of oil. Not surprisingly, countries like Saudi Arabia do not lodge all their foreign assets with their central banks. They do not treat all of those assets as reserves.

Setting aside this special nonmonetary case, the justifications for holding reserves and for changes in reserves derive directly from the fact that the float is not clean. Governments intervene in foreign-exchange markets to affect the course of the exchange rates. In fact, countries are distributed today all along the spectrum of exchange-rate regimes, from virtual fixity all the way to fairly clean floating. To make matters more complicated, some countries fix their rates in terms of a single foreign currency; others fix them in terms of a basket of currencies, including the SDR; and some have so-called gliding parities, which mandate changes in exchange rates fairly frequently but by small amounts.

Even among the so-called floaters, the extent of intervention varies tremendously from country to country, and it has varied hugely across time. I take, for example, the case of the United Kingdom. The Bank of England was active in exchange markets until fairly recently, but it is intervening much less now and is thus allowing the exchange rate to respond freely to British economic policies and to exogenous disturbances affecting Britain's external accounts.

The members of the European Monetary System are, of course, a special case. Their exchange rates are more or less fixed internally, but they are not fixed externally. They do, however, intervene extensively to influence exchange rates with outsiders' currencies, especially the U.S. dollar.

Under the old Bretton Woods system, reserve changes were the first indicators of shifts in demand or supply in foreign-exchange markets. There was then some clear sense in which the size of reserve holdings, country by country and globally as well, had to grow gradually, along with the sizes of disturbances affecting demands and supplies in foreign-exchange markets. As Robert Heller reminds us, moreover, reserve holdings had to bear some plausible relationship to the speed with which national economies could be expected to adjust to external disturbances.

There was also a clear sense, at least in surplus countries, that actual reserve accumulation was governed by the policies of deficit countries, especially the policies of the United States, whose currency had become the main reserve asset. In the simple models that were built to describe the reserve system, the supply of reserves was determined by the U.S. balance-of-payments deficit and was thus determined primarily by the macro-economic policies of the United States. It was known that this was not entirely true, because the policies of other countries affected the U.S. balance of payments, but it was useful nonetheless to emphasize the strategic role of the United States.

It was quite clear in any case that reserve accumulation reflected the commitment to keep exchange rates fixed, and that is no longer true. Under present circumstances, reserve accumulation reflects the exercise of an option, not the fulfillment of a commitment. Governments are entirely free to decide whether to intervene in the exchange market, whether or not to allow a disturbance affecting the demand for a country's currency to be absorbed by changing the supply and thus changing its reserves or by permitting the exchange rate to change.

There has been some work by academics on the optimal division of responses to disturbances, as between changes in reserves and exchange rates. But the state of our knowledge is primitive, partly because our models are far too simple. Most of them start out by assuming that any change in reserves is reflected immediately and completely in the money supply of the country concerned—that there is no sterilization of reserve changes. That is manifestly false in both the short term and the long term. Some of our models, moreover, rule out whole classes of disturbances and important classes of response to disturbances. Models of this type impose continuous purchasing-power parity and, therefore, exclude expenditure-switching disturbances as well as expenditure-switching changes in real exchange rates. Finally, models concerned with optimal responses necessarily assume that the monetary authorities can distinguish among types of disturbances affecting the demand for a country's currency, just as we assume in much of the rest of our work that private participants in foreign-exchange markets know enough to form rational expectations. These assumptions are naive.

Basically, then, the reserve system is quite different today, and our understanding of the system is as yet quite limited, compared with what it was a few years ago.

There is one aspect of the system that has not changed in recent years, and it needs to be emphasized. The form in which reserves accrue to any single country is determined, as it always has been, by that country's choice of intervention currency. That important choice, in turn, is determined primarily by the way that foreign-exchange markets are organized.

Do not forget, however, that our discussion has centered on the industrial countries. Most of the developing countries continue to peg their exchange rates and, therefore, view the reserve system in traditional terms. They will continue to have a need for reserves related to the sizes of disturbances confronting them, although we cannot calculate that need as finely as we once pretended.

Returning to the main theme, I can summarize by saying that the reserve-supply process, the way in which reserves accrue, is not neatly controllable. It used to be controlled to a first approximation by the size of the U.S. balance-of-payments deficit and by SDR creation. But the stock of reserves is determined today by the sum of the separate decisions of all countries in the system, decisions concerning intervention in foreign-exchange markets. Reserves grow whenever countries intervene. It is extremely difficult, therefore, to develop and apply criteria for SDR creation.

The present situation is complicated enormously by the fact that countries can intervene not only by using reserves but also by borrowing from Eurocurrency markets. They can likewise build up reserves by borrowing to hold reserves against some future calamity.

Some say, incidentally, that the growth of borrowing in Eurocurrency markets has reduced the need for growth in global reserves. True enough, but something must be added. Countries that have borrowed and are deeply in debt may need more reserves now, because they cannot continue to borrow, and because they must be able to persuade their creditors that they can repay. Reserve positions may become increasingly important in their effects on the judgments of creditors about the propriety of extending new loans and rolling over old ones.

Under the Bretton Woods system, there was very little concern about the composition of international reserves, apart from the issue of gold-dollar convertibility. Among currencies, at least, the dollar was deemed to be as good as any. In consequence, reserves that accrued as dollars, because the dollar was the main intervention currency, were then held in dollars, because the dollar was regarded as the preeminent reserve currency.

With the movement to floating exchange rates, the situation changed, although the change took place with a long lag. Comprehensive figures are hard to come by, but those that I have seen suggest that the deutsche mark now accounts for about 15 percent of the currency reserves held by central-banks governments; other currencies, apart from the dollar, account for about 10 percent, and the share of the dollar has thus fallen to about 75 percent of total reserve-currency holdings. If one were to take out the reserve holdings of the major reserve centers and look only at countries that are free to diversify, because their own currencies are not reserve currencies, the share of the dollar would be about 50 percent, if not lower.

Reserve diversification by central banks—the movement out of the dollar—has not been the major cause of the recent turbulence in foreign-exchange markets, but it has not been a trivial phenomenon either, and anticipations of central-bank sales may have been important in triggering movements of private funds.

Two phenomena need attention here. The first is the diversification of reserve stocks—the once-and-for-all movement out of the dollar that has taken place and may be complete by now. The second is the process alluded to earlier. Reserves continue to accrue in dollars, because of intervention conducted in dollars, and there is thus the possibility of continuing tension in the system. The currency in which reserves accrue is not the one in which countries will want to invest all of their new reserves. Even if the diversification of the existing stock of reserves has gone as far as it is likely to go, the system may be plagued by an ongoing problem, focused on the dollar, insofar as countries continue to acquire dollar reserves and want to diversify those acquisitions.

Reserve diversification has produced a multiple-reserve-asset system, and we have been told that such a system is dangerous because it is inherently unstable. Such a system poses worrisome problems, but the popular phrase ''inherently unstable'' exaggerates those problems because the phrase evokes a false analogy.

It evokes an analogy with a bimetallic system or the old gold-dollar system in which the prices of the main reserve assets were fixed in terms of one another. Under systems with fixed prices, holders of reserves can switch freely from one asset to another, and they can speculate against the system without exposing themselves to large losses. If their reserve holdings are big enough, they can bring down the system.

Because the prices of the principal reserve assets are not fixed today, there may be a self-limiting or stabilizing element in the system. A multiple-reserve-asset system may be far less unstable than its fixed-price predecessors.

Nevertheless, the new system imposes obligations on the reserve centers, and I am not entirely sure that the new reserve-currency countries are prepared to assume those obligations. Last year, we witnessed a significant change in the attitude of Germany, which now appears more willing to allow the use of its currency as a reserve asset. The permanence of that change, however, is doubtful. Is Germany really interested in a larger reserve role for the deutsche mark, or is the recent change of view a reflection of the short-term need to finance a large current-account deficit?

There are two ways of responding to the problems posed by reserve diversification. The first approach can be characterized as damage limitation. It is to accept and consolidate the multiple-reserve-asset system by negotiating ways of stabilizing it beyond what markets can do unaided. It may be appropriate, for example, to coordinate more formally the intervention policies of the reserve centers. It may be necessary to coordinate their monetary policies in order to make their currencies equally attractive as reserve assets, at least to avoid competition among them in attracting reserve balances.

The second approach would seek to limit diversification, even to reverse it, by restricting the freedom of reserve holders to change their portfolios. Many holders, we are told, would not accept this sort of regulation without some quid pro quo, but sooner or later restrictions may be needed, to stabilize the new reserve system.

12 Central-Bank Optimization in the Holdings of Foreign-Exchange Reserves

David Lomax

The role of the commercial banks—in the context discussed in this chapter—is somewhat different from that of the government and the international organizations. I think President Kennedy coined the phrase "an idealist without illusions"; it is not the job of the commercial banks to reform the system. Their job is to understand the system and to operate it. Even though bankers do have ideals and occasionally, illusions, my task here is to talk about how I see the system actually working and what I think are the benefits or merits of the present way of going about things.

If there is a major theme in this chapter, it is that, in the marketplace, countries and asset holders are trying to solve their own problems, to optimize their own situation. One has a situation of suboptimizing by central banks, investment organizations, and the like. The reasons these organizations choose the policies they do is of particular interest.

One has to pay considerable respect to their view of their own problems and the way they decide their policies on asset holding. There are two ways of looking at this international situation. On the one hand the system can be viewed from the center, and one has to be concerned with the whole system. On the other hand, almost all systems must allow optimizing at the lower level of its various components. One thus poses the question: Under what circumstances can one say that this optimizing by individual agencies is too harmful to be allowed to continue? How should suboptimizing by nations and by investment organizations be reconciled with the constraints imposed by the system as a whole?

As far as national-reserve asset management is concerned, there are a very large number of objectives and constraints that countries have to bear in mind. One is the value of their reserves. What is their target in terms of the value of their reserves? Is it maximizing it? Is it avoiding a substantial fall in reserve value? Second, there is the income to be generated from their reserves. How important is that? Third, there is the question of hedging; a certain amount of discussion of this is necessary because a large number of countries are in fact in deficit in the international financial markets, and their asset policy is strongly linked to their liability policy or the liabilities they have. The corresponding matching of these two risks is important.

A fourth point is justification. Most central bankers wish to keep their jobs, and deciding the policy on the reserve management of a particular country is a sensitive matter that has to be decided within the political framework of the government, and there must be policy papers saying what the objective is. Having a defensible reserve-asset policy is a very important feature for a large number of countries and for central bankers.

A further constraint is the availability of assets. Countries may have certain liabilities but be unable to have the assets they would like because they are not available in the marketplace. Another feature of a country's reserve assets that was mentioned previously in this book is the question of the overall size that is desired.

Toward the end of this chapter, some remarks are made about how the exchange market actually functions and how the behavior of countries in these markets affects its volatility or otherwise. At the end of the chapter there is discussion of the SDR, particularly the new SDR, and how this might fit in with further developments of the system.

In almost all countries reserve-asset policy is kept well clear of public and political debate. Canada is perhaps an exception, in that it publishes a fairly informative document about its reserve-asset policy, but in most countries there is no public discussion about this issue. The reserve composition is not normally published. The valuation of reserves often is not published, and the objectives of reserve policy are also in many cases not made explicit in public debate. The income from reserves is normally not a major feature of the national income of the country concerned.

In many countries the reserves cover only two or three months' imports, so an interest rate of about 10 percent on the reserves is equivalent to about the value of nine days' imports. If, for example, one gained an extra 1 percent on the income of the reserves by clever management, one would gain about an extra day's import value. This is not a vast amount of money, and one does not see great pressure on countries to maximize the income from their reserve assets.

As one talks to central bankers and treasury ministers about their reserve policy one receives a variety of answers incorporating a range of criteria. Some governments talk about preserving the real value of their reserves and others about maximizing, but in fact the structure of reserves is often based on political and other conventions. Canada, for example, keeps its reserves almost entirely in dollars, apart from its gold holdings, as part of its package deal with the United States.

The Group of Ten countries keep their reserves almost entirely in dollars. If they were to hold each other's currencies, they would just swap currencies and the situation would be more out of hand and not to their own particular desire.

One has much wider diversification of reserves for the developing countries. As Peter Kenen said, the U.S. dollar share of currency reserves is about 75 percent now, or less than 75 percent. If one takes out the reserves of the Group of Ten countries themselves, the dollar component for the other countries is probably not much more than half, if as large as that.

The question of justification for reserve policy was raised earlier in the chapter. If one adopts a policy of maximizing reserves, then of course one has the possibility of failure. One theme that emerges from a thorough examination of the behavior of asset holders and national asset holders is that of extreme caution. Central banks have to get their treasuries to accept a policy for the management of the reserve assets, and a key feature of the views put forth by central banks is one that minimizes the possibility that they will be forced to go back to the treasury some months later and say "we have failed." This points toward diversification and toward a defensible policy that cannot be tested too severely in terms of the profit and loss on the transactions.

On the hedging point, some countries say they hold assets to the same value of their liabilities in certain hard currencies, but then hold the balance of their assets in dollars. Others try to match their reserves to their trading composition. Some try to match their reserves to the composition of their public debt or guaranteed debt, but ignore the liabilities of the corporate and private sector.

If one were doing a foreign-exchange exposure study for a country, it would be very difficult to ask precisely what liabilities should be taken in conjunction with the assets to build up the proper exposure pattern. Should one include long-and short-term debt? Should one include all the assets of the public sector?

If one takes the example of Canada, where the provinces are allowed to have external assets as well as considerable flexibility in their borrowing policy through the international markets, the central government has no real control over either the assets of the nation externally or the liabilities even of the public sector. Similar considerations apply in Australia, which is a federal country, where the timing and the choice of markets when the states borrow is something over which the federal government has relatively little control.

One also has the factor in many cases that the borrowing organizations within a country may have a system for hedging the liability that takes place within that particular market or that particular financial contract and, therefore, not rely upon the central government to do the hedging for them.

Externally financing a coal project in, say, one of the states of Australia is a good case in point. The coal price is similar to energy prices, which presumably are in some ways linked to the outlook of the world economy, and, therefore, the export price to be obtained in the future from this project may in some way be regarded or constructed to be a hedge against the liability of the project. It might not, therefore, be regarded as a responsibility of the central government to hedge this particular contract.

The point to be stressed is that the vast majority of countries today—almost all, if one excludes the Group of Ten countries and the few OPEC asset holders—are net liability holders on the world financial markets, and, therefore, the matching of their liabilities is a key feature and not a very easy one with which to formulate assets.

On the question of the value of the reserve assets one hears rather loose talk about structurally strong currencies and structurally weak currencies. The pressure toward diversification of reserve assets developed very heavily toward 1978 as countries saw the long slide in the value of the dollar, and at that point many countries began to diversify their reserve assets quite strongly into a wide range of other currencies, in some cases on the view that the other currencies were structurally strong.

In fact, if one could look at the information in detail in many central banks, one would find that this particular policy turned out to be mistaken, and many countries have in fact either taken losses or have earned less income than if they had stayed in dollars over the last couple of years.

This brings up a point made earlier in this book. Central banks of countries around the world are not necessarily particularly informed. They do not have the power to move exchange rates the way they may want to do so. Based on the behavior of exchange rates over the past couple of years, one must conclude that most of these countries are really concerned with diversification as a point of principle, and the stress on maximizing has lessened, given the experience they had in the marketplace.

Just to give an example: Insofar as I have become involved in trying to help manage funds for certain countries, the policy of asset holders is to divide their long-term portfolio into a large number of small portfolios and then decide the currency composition of each of those portfolios. Then they may give each of these little segments to a certain bank or similar segments to two or three different banks to run. They will try to get some maximizing out of this by having two banks given similar portfolios and test which one does better and thus give them an incentive to change the contract, and so on.

The underlying effect of this kind of behavior is simply one of diversifying and avoiding maximum loss, and this gives very little choice indeed over the deportment of the funds in any very significant way.

Some central banks take the view that they are very capable and smart operators, and one could say that they have dynamic and determined policies genuinely to do the best they can in the marketplace. Perhaps the classic example of this is the Singapore Monetary Authority, and other South Asian central banks have pursued similar policies; but not all that many central banks are willing to take the risk and apply such determination to the management of their reserve assets.

Other central banks claim that they maximize the value of their reserves, but I doubt very much if that is exactly what they mean. They mean maximizing within very tightly set down constraints.

A part of reserve policy is the question of liquidity. Liquidity is required primarily for the sake of running the exchange market, and that applies to all countries, whether developing or developed. But having liquidity is a way of buying time and a way of not having to be forced to do things you do not want to do because the market gives you no choice. The amount of liquidity that countries have depends or should depend on the volatility and the risk-taking that they are facing in this particular matter, and clearly a country with very volatile export earnings or, perhaps, with volatile import requirements would have more liquidity than a country with a more stable development of its inflows and outflows.

In most cases the amount of liquidity held by countries not on a maximizing basis is very large, and one is surprised by the conservatism of the overall portfolio structure of the reserve assets of a country when viewed against, say, the question of whether they should be trying to make as much money as possible out of it.

Some countries use banks extensively in managing their reserve assets; there are three main features of this. In some cases countries actually use banks as managers of their internal cash flow and their budget. This happens in the case of countries that have had very severe domestic internal administrative problems, and there is the troika of merchant banks that do this very complex job in relation to the management of reserve assets. The second level is that some countries use banks in order to determine their strategy in sorting out and deciding reserve-asset policy, currencies, maturities, and so on. The third level of this relationship is when countries use banks simply to manage particular defined portfolios that they have set up in the way that was described earlier. They will possibly have twenty or thirty or forty different portfolios based on maturity and currency and then have banks on contract managing these particular features.

There are two contrasting trends in this area of national policy. On the one hand, the sophistication and experience of the central banks in managing reserve assets has undoubtedly increased enormously over the past decade or so, and the ability and skill applied in these areas is very substantial indeed. On the other hand, the amount of reserves being accumulated by some countries has been increasing so enormously—and obviously Saudi Arabia and other OPEC countries are the classic examples—that in this case the sheer scale of the money has led to a greater degree of contracting in order to take some of the load off the actual central-government organization itself.

I mentioned earlier that the vast majority of countries, including those in Europe, are not net-liability holders, and in these countries the reserve policy is a key feature in maintaining the country's creditworthiness. The great majority of countries attach the maximum importance to retaining their creditworthiness in the world financial markets, which are the source of large amounts of financial resources for them, on terms that, provided they can maintain creditworthiness, are not too conditional—not too strongly conditions—as far as they are concerned.

As is well known, the normal system is for commercial organizations, the banks and the bond market, to assess countries on the basis of certain ratios. These are not an exact science, but most organizations tend to use similar criteria. One has the debt-service ratio, the ratio of debt to exports, the ratio of debt to GNP, the number of months' imports covered by reserves, and other similar calculations.

As described earlier in the book much of the borrowing that took place up to 1979 was used to build up reserves—on the quite correct assumption that when economic circumstances and borrowing conditions became more difficult a country with substantial reserves would have a larger period of time in which to take decisions on its future policy. Decisions to build up reserves for this cautionary purpose have clearly been vindicated in a large number of cases.

If one takes the example of Brazil, they will probably have reduced their reserves by $5 billion in 1980 in relation to their total net borrowing needs of something like $10-$12 billion. Had the reserves not been built up to about $10 billion, then they would have had to take much harder decisions, much earlier, on their entire economic program.

One can argue that they may have taken too long anyway to take these decisions, but from their own point of view and given the sensitivity of domestic politics to the changes in decisions, having the reserves was a key element of their strategy.

There are, in fact, various potential clashes between policy objectives as regards reserves and creditworthiness. If a country borrows to increase its reserves, at the same time it clearly increases the ratios of debt to exports and the debt-service ratio while at the same time improving the ratio of reserves to imports, the import-coverage ratio.

If a country is getting near the borderline of conventional criteria of creditworthiness, then there can be a carefully calculated trade-off between the benefits of borrowing to increase reserves and, at the same time, the adverse effect upon the other ratios that the country has in mind. It cannot be overemphasized that this calculation is of the most vital importance to countries, given the great importance they attach to access to the commercial markets.

We turn now to the foreign-exchange markets and make the possible use of the SDR. The foreign-exchange market is basically like a capital market. The leverage that can be applied to an exchange rate by financial flows is a colossal multiple of the current-account flows going across an exchange market or of the long-term capital flows. One has to consider that even with exchange control in most foreign-exchange markets or most countries it would be legal to lead or lag imports and exports up to six months; the amount of money, then, that could cross an exchange market in a day would be some phenomenal multiple of the normal trading volume on that particular day.

It is also like a capital market in that expectations about the future play an enormous role in the flows taking place on a particular day. The number of transactions in the marketplace each day is huge, and every transaction is largely of a financial character, in which the people who take the decision are saying, "What is the cost of this transaction in terms of interest differentials, and what is the expectation of the exchange rate moving over the period of the transaction so as to either increase my profit or make this transaction turn into a loss"? The vast majority of participants in these markets, and of governments for that matter, are heavily risk averse and relatively cautious.

Whether one likes these characteristics or not, this is how one really has to see the market. These characteristics in themselves are quite sufficient to give foreign-exchange markets a certain brittle quality. These characteristics of the market can be fully accounted for by its own structure, by the behavior pattern of the participants, and by the financial flows generated in the marketplace.

The increased role of governments and central banks in these markets does not make that much of a difference. The short-term volatility of the marketplace is determined by varying conditions; central banks are only one factor.

Central banks are not particularly wise. They are not better than the market in making decisions; they are just like any other asset holder. Therefore, it is hard to prove the point that what they do in the market will really affect the flows dramatically in the short term and therefore make it more volatile. Certainly my own very limited experience of trying to be involved in managing reserves or helping to manage reserves indicates the extreme of caution and nervousness one applies in these situations, and the lack of aggressive moves one makes that might have the effect of swinging exchange rates quite dramatically.

In other words, the marketplace is the market, and it cannot be said that countries taking part in managing their reserves really make it much more volatile in the short term.

On the question of the SDR, there is a certain amount of hope that the SDR will be used more actively in the marketplace. As stated earlier in this chapter, the currency composition chosen by countries is based in many cases on a very complicated calculation of their requirements, hedging, and trade links. The vast majority of countries, then, probably would not choose the actual composition of the SDR as their optimum asset mix.

The SDR becomes, therefore, an option either through the IMF substitution account or through the marketplace, and as an option there are quite significant hopes. National Westminister Bank and many other banks have been offering SDR deposits in the marketplace in recent months. It is only because of modern computer technology that one can do this now. We have a multicolored video machine that is the delight and joy of our foreign-exchange dealing room. If it was not for the extreme skill of computing these days, the old-sixteen currency SDR could hardly be used in an actual foreign-exchange trading environment. But it has been used, and it was developed by us at the insistence of an asset-holding country that wanted to place such deposits; it has been proved quite feasible.

With the five-currency SDR the picture changes dramatically. There is no reason at all why commercial organizations should not be able to offer deposits in five-currency SDRs as proper banking transactions. The currencies are all marketable up to three months or a year. There is a very long deposit market in most of these currencies, and in the forward market it is certainly active up to a year and longer in some particular cases.

The degree of skill required to use the SDR in the financial market is now well within the competence of the vast majority of banks dealing in the international foreign-exchange markets, and one sees no reason that, as the demand for deposits builds up, this should not take place.

If the IMF does in fact come into the commercial markets they will wish to borrow SDRs, for a variety of reasons; banks, therefore, will have this excellent credit risk to lend to in SDRs, and this will enhance the use of the currency both within the commercial markets and in general public discussion.

Once the SDR becomes a practical feature of the financing scene it will also be used for one other reason. The SDR is a very defensible mix to use on behalf of an asset holder. If you are a central-bank governor and you wish to defend to your finance minister your choice of asset mix, it is acceptable just to say you have chosen the SDR. If you use some other asset mix you have to say why, and if you get it wrong you have to give the reason why you chose it.

In conclusion, I would just like to say from my worm's eye view of the scene that one sees that countries seem to be making a very serious effort to solve their own problems. It is very hard to see why countries should not be allowed to solve their own problems, and the question that comes up is the balance between the requirements of the system and the feeling that countries have that they must help themselves to optimize their own solutions and to see how that fits in with the rest of the financial system.

13 Managing Exchange Rates and International Reserves

William Hood

Introduction

This chapter focuses on the implications for the managing of exchange rates and reserves of two dominant features of the scene. The significance these features seem to have for the International Monetary Fund will also be discussed. The two features are (1) the diffusion of power and (2) the concentration of surpluses. The former is a slower-moving evolutionary process; the latter came upon us more suddenly.

The phrase "the diffusion of power" refers to the process by which the United States has increasingly shared with other major industrial countries the preeminent economic and political strength it achieved following World War II. There was a period of about two decades—one should not try to define it too precisely—during which the position of the United States in the world economy was predominant. During this period the strength of the British economy was further drained. In both Europe and Japan the recovery from war took time, and until that recovery was solidly established the economic supremacy of the United States in the West was unchallenged.

Now, we are in a transition phase. Speaking only of the noncommunist world, the economic strength formerly concentrated in the United States is being shared increasingly with Western Europe, Japan, and the newly emerging industrial nations. It was against the background of U.S. economic supremacy that the systems of management of exchange reserves and rates that served during the postwar period were established. The evolution of the structure of economic power has brought and probably will continue to bring important changes in the management of exchange reserves and rates.

Of more recent origin, but contributing significantly to these changes, has been the concentration of balance-of-payments surpluses in the oil-producing countries. This development represents a special aspect of the dispersion of power. It does not, however, have to be thought of in that context, for rather independently and in its own right it has affected and continues to affect management practices in respect to exchange rates and reserves.

The impact of these two broad features of the evolving world scene on the management of exchange rates and reserves by national authorities will be discussed in turn; discussion of the impact on the approach of the IMF to rate and reserve management concludes the chapter.

Consequences of the Diffusion of Power

When the United States was the dominant economic power, it made a great deal of sense for countries of the rest of the world to operate on what was in effect a dollar standard and to maintain their currencies in a fixed relationship to the dollar. The proportion of world trade that was focused on the United States was high. The currency in which the trade was denominated was the dollar. The United States provided banking services to the world—not uniquely but increasingly; it provided long-term capital; it provided the exchange reserves that the rest of the world needed. A fixed exchange-rate system centered on the dollar suited the concentration of economic power that then prevailed.

The breakup of the fixed-rate system, centered upon the dollar, had many contributing causes. But at root was the changing distribution of economic power. This diffusion of power made the arguments for a system based on the dollar less compelling. It also added political force to the moves toward a more open system. The breakup of the fixed-rate system, then, was one of the major consequences of the diffusion of economic power.

This development brought in its train a number of important changes in the management of the rate and reserves. With the establishing of floating rates, the United States has adopted a rather different attitude toward the management of its exchange rate. In an earlier day, the U.S. authorities felt more keenly the responsibility to defend the relationship of the dollar to gold than to defend the relationships that other countries had established of their currencies to the dollar. Accordingly, the authorities only rarely intervened in the exchange markets for the purpose of affecting the rate. Today, management of the rate in the form of direct market intervention is a much more normal occurrence for the United States.

For countries other than the United States, of course, direct intervention in the exchange market has been a normal procedure. In the management of the rate from day to day, intervention to maintain orderly conditions is as much a policy of a floating-rate regime as of a fixed-rate regime. Some very sophisticated arrangements to provide mutual support and prevent conflict have been developed in recent years within the European Monetary System (EMS), discussed later in the chapter, and outside of the EMS as well. But as far as dollar exchange rates are concerned, management is less directed to the control of the periodic crises that came to be the hallmark of the fixed-rate system. The exchange rate can be allowed to take a greater share of the pressures, and of course this puts less pressure on authorities to husband their reserves. It is sometimes alleged that this implies less discipline upon countries in conducting their domestic policies. Without entering this debate, it can still be asserted that, at least among the older industrialized countries, the concern with the exchange rate is so much less under a floating regime that the wish to influence it or manage it through general monetary and fiscal policies is markedly less than under a fixed-rate regime. But it does appear to be the case that the concentration of management effort on the resolution of crises is much less under the floating system.

Regarding the management of reserves, we will look first at the United States. Although the United States continued to maintain the convertibility of the U.S. dollar to gold at $35 per ounce, the U.S. authorities had to pay attention to the size of its gold stock in relation to the demands that might be made upon it. With the growth in the volume of U.S. dollars held in the reserves of others, the ratio of U.S. dollars held by foreign monetary authorities to the gold held by the United States continued to rise, and this became, of course, a cause of concern. But of more practical importance were changes in the willingness of foreign holders to hold U.S. dollars. There were many factors playing upon this willingness, but underlying them all was the relative economic strength of the United States. As this changed the willingness to hold the dollar in reserves declined; reserve management, in the sense of programs to reduce the balance-of-payments deficit so as to reduce the buildup of U.S. dollars held in reserves abroad as well as programs to deter U.S. dollar holders from claiming gold, became very active. Although it is not necessary to review that history, we should contrast these approaches to reserve management with those in evidence in the United States today. The concern with gold is of a much different kind. Indeed, the United States has recently deliberately sold gold from its stock. The United States now has to ensure that it has access to sufficient quantities of foreign currencies to finance any acquisition of U.S. dollars in the exchange markets that it may wish to undertake. We may note that the readiness of the United States to hold currencies in its reserves in and of itself represents some diversification of total reserve holdings by currency.

But it is not only the United States that has sought to hold other currencies in its reserves. Other countries have moved to diversify the denominations of their foreign-currency reserves. One must not exaggerate the extent of this change. The SDR value of the U.S. dollar share in official holdings of foreign exchange fell from its peak of 87 percent at the end of 1976 to 65 percent at the end of 1979 (or 79 percent if one regards European Currency Units (ECUs) issued against dollars as dollars and if one deducts from the total all ECUs issued against gold). The change is significant, however, and it has occurred against a background of a very very large increase in the total of foreign-currency holdings in official reserves and, until recently, a considerable resistance on the part of countries such as Germany and Japan whose currencies have been sought for reserve holding.

To summarize, then, the diffusion of power that has been going on in the world has produced some very notable changes in the management of reserves and exchange rates. It basically underlies the breakup of the fixed-rate system, so that what is being managed now is a complex system of floating rates between the dollar and the various major currencies. It has brought the United States into the currency market rather than the gold market in the management of U.S. dollar rates. It has changed the U.S. concern from one of protecting the gold stock in reserves to one of ensuring that access to foreign currencies is adequate for its operations. It has led other countries to start to diversify their increasing foreign-currency reserves. But this is not all; the diffusion of power has led to a general atmosphere of instability, which in its turn has led to a series of defensive actions affecting the management of rates and reserves.

When, in history, a particular country has a superiority of economic power, then so long as it exercises that power, and the concomitant political power, in a manner to inspire confidence, the economic system can enjoy a measure of stability that it is often denied in other circumstances. For a time in the postwar period, U.S. dominance in the economic sphere provided that kind of stability. But with the growing strength of other nations, and some impairment of competitiveness and growth rates in the United States, economic power became more dispersed, and the United States could no longer offer this stability. An illustration of the types of instability that ensued follows.

When power is less concentrated there may be at times a general sense of the absence of orderliness simply because power is less concentrated and therefore less visible. In these circumstances adverse developments may be more prone to excite expectations of a deteriorating situation and more prone, therefore, to lead to deterioration.

A further generalization is of importance. It is well established that the more equally power is dispersed among a small group of interacting bodies, the more unstable is likely to be the relationship among them. For example, there probably exists in the present circumstances of diffused power greater likelihood that one country will feel that its efforts at achieving policy objectives are frustrated by policy actions of other countries. Consider the great debate of a year or so ago when enormous pressure was placed upon Germany and Japan to expand their economies so as to increase their imports, moderate the increase in the exchange values of their currencies, and give the deficit countries greater scope for expanding their growth without adding to domestic inflationary pressures.

From Europe from time to time we have heard complaints that U.S. interest rates were too low, the inflation rate too high, the current-account deficit too high, and the financing of it through the issue of U.S. dollar liabilities damaging to European monetary objectives. More recently the argument has run the other way: U.S. inflation is too high but interest rates are also, and this is unsettling to certain European policy objectives.

Beyond these more general considerations certain more specific matters creating uncertainty and instability may be cited. The floating rates have shown more movement than was the case during the years when power was concentrated and the world was basically on a fixed-rate system. During the breakup of the exchange-rate systems, of course, periods of great exchange-rate instability marking adjustments of par values punctuated intervals of rate stability. (Incidentally, the intervals of rate stability exhibited a good deal of reserve instability.)

Since the breakup of the exchange-rate system, there has not been this crisis pattern, but there has been a considerable variability of rates. For example, we calculate that in June 1980 the effective exchange rate of the deutsche mark was 30 percent above its 1975 level, while that of the lira was more than 30 percent below its 1975 level. The effective rate of the yen went from some 110 percent of its 1975 level in 1977 to nearly 160 percent toward the end of 1978 and back to about 115 percent in April 1980. Focusing now on volatility, measured by the standard deviation of monthly percentage changes in the effective rate about the average percentage change during the year, we find a considerable variation from country to country and from year to year. It is difficult to say that a clear trend is evident here, one way or the other, but the variability itself—as well as the variability of the variability—may well be an unsettling feature of the current scene. It is necessary to discuss the instabilities associated with the growing dispersion of power because these very instabilities generate pressures to coordinate approaches to problems or to form coalitions to meet problems.

Two examples follow, both of which continue to be relevant to the management of exchange rates and reserves today. The first example—the establishing of the federal-reserve swap network—comes from the period when the fixed-rate system was first threatened. Here was a cooperative effort to permit monetary authorities to acquire access to foreign reserves at a moment's notice in order to influence exchange rates indirectly, by showing larger reserves, or directly, through intervention. This cooperative effort was a response to instability. There were many other examples of this kind that were developed during the instability of the breakup of the exchange-rate system. Not all of them, such as the gold-pool arrangements, had reason to survive to the present period.

The second example is the setting up of the European Monetary System, which entered into force in March 1979. There were many forces leading to the setting up of the EMS; many false starts were made before success was achieved. Among the forces at work, and without which the scheme would not have gone forward, were the reactions against the lack of U.S. economic leadership and the instabilities consequent upon the diffusion of economic power. Without detailing the functioning of the EMS, let it be acknowledged that its existence materially affects the management of exchange rates and reserves in the world, particularly on the part of its members.

Discussion of how the reactions to the diffusion of power have affected the IMF and its manner of operating, occurs later in the chapter. We turn our attention first to the implications of the concentration of surpluses for the management of rates and reserves.

Consequences of the Concentration of Surpluses

Regarding management of rates, it is common knowledge that the theory of the working of the balance-of-payments adjustment mechanism envisages that countries in balance-of-payments deficit to a degree beyond that which is capable of being financed on a sustainable basis should adjust that deficit by a variety of means, including a decline in the external value of its currency. Equally, a country in surplus should participate in the adjustment process and certainly should allow its exchange rate to appreciate as the counterpart to the devaluation of the deficit countries.

A curiosity of the present situation with the surplus concentrated in the oil-exporting countries is that there is very little argument to the effect that the oil producers should increase the external value of their currencies in order to adjust their imbalance of payments. The producers argue that they are raising the price of their imports to do just that and, in addition, cannot absorb imports at a more rapid rate. The consumers of oil argue that they do not want the producers to sell less oil until they, the consumers, are prepared for the shifts of energy resources and energy uses that they inevitably have to make. Of course, among the oil-consuming countries, payments imbalances continue, and there continues to be a role for exchange-rate movements in adjusting the degree of imbalance among these countries.

Exchange-rate movements among the industrial countries have been substantial. In 1980 the degree of exchange-market intervention by the major countries appears to have increased and the volatility of exchange rates may have been somewhat dampened. One might surmise, in the circumstances of generalized deficits originating in substantial measure from a common cause that by common consent cannot be removed by exchange-rate action, that there may well be less readiness than might otherwise be the case to promote actively balance-of-payments adjustment through exchange-rate management.

Our discussion now returns to the implications of the concentration of surpluses for the management of reserves. The concentration of surpluses has contributed to a very large increase in reserves, especially in the foreign-exchange component. Dealings in oil are very largely in terms of U.S. dollars, and the trade in oil therefore results largely in the first instance in an increase in U.S. dollar reserves.

From the end of 1973 to the end of May 1980, the foreign-exchange component of international reserves as measured in SDRs increased from about 100 billion to 260 billion. Of this SDR 160 billion increase, about one-fifth accrued to nonoil developing countries, one-half accrued to industrial countries, and the remaining three-tenths stayed in the reserves of the oil producers. Oil deficits did not generate all of the creation of currency reserves, but they accounted for a good part of it. As the reserves were recycled, they spread about the system. It is worth noting that for a time some nonoil developing countries were borrowing in excess of their current deficits and building up reserves. So the first implication is that the concentration of surpluses produced a very much larger volume of reserves to manage.

One could now proceed to discuss the whole recycling issue in its various aspects. This will not be undertaken here, but mention must be made of the fact that the management of their reserves by the oil-producing countries has contributed to the diversification of holdings by currency noted earlier.

In concluding this section it can be said that some countries that had shown a reluctance to issue liabilities denominated in their currencies have shown less reluctance as their need to finance deficits grew. Yen-denominated bonds or deutsche mark-denominated bonds issued to the oil producers may or may not all be shown in oil-producers' reserves, but by using their dollar reserves they have acquired capital assets denominated in other currencies.

**Impact of the Diffusion of Power
and Concentration of Deficits on the IMF's
Approach to Exchange Rates and Reserves**

The IMF is very much concerned with the managing of exchange rates and of reserves. The most important implication of the diffusion of power is the general one that the instability associated with the diffusing and later diffusion of power induces countries to turn to institutions such as the Fund to help provide the orderliness or stability that is lacking.

One could argue that the very idea of creating the Fund was a delayed reaction (delayed by World War II) to the instabilities of the 1930s. One might also note that the Fund was not a particularly active organization during many years when U.S. economic power was dominant in the first part of the postwar period.

However, as the diffusion of power progressed, the movement for reform of the system grew. The Fund was intimately involved in that movement. The idea of the SDR as an alternative reserve asset comprising of a composite of currencies was born and brought to reality. The first allocation of SDRs was made on 1 January 1970. The Fund became more active as a provider of balance-of-payments support. Quotas were increased on several occasions. The seventh increase is about to become effective, and work on the eighth review is commencing. The extended Fund Facility began in 1974 and the Supplementary Financing Facility in 1977. But perhaps the most significant development arising out of this period was the confirmation of floating as an accepted exchange-rate practice for Fund members in the revision of the Fund's Articles agreed in Jamaica in 1976 and the companion injunction to the Fund to "exercise firm surveillance over the exchange rate policies of members and [to] adopt specific principles for the guidance of all members with respect to those policies." The Fund has adopted these principles (1977) and has been evolving its procedures for surveillance.

The concentration of surpluses has led to a number of specific responses of the Fund that have affected the management of reserves and rates. The Oil Facilities, the Trust Fund, the Subsidy Account, and the Gold Sales Policy are good examples. But these are now passing into history.

The more recent events include the extension of the conditional amounts that the Fund is willing to provide in relation to a country's quota. The Fund has taken the view that the oil deficits require financing over rather longer periods of time than have been normal in Fund financing, in order to permit structural adjustments to be made in members' economies. The Fund expects that a very large proportion of the required financing of deficits will continue to be provided by the private institutions, but it stands ready to help on a scale unprecedented in its history.

To finance this greater activity, the Fund will have to borrow funds. This borrowing will provide SDR-denominated assets. To some extent these assets will permit diversification of reserves into SDRs. This, together with the continuing and perhaps increased allocations of SDRs and the growing reserve positions in the general account of the Fund, may provide in a limited way the opportunity for diversification of reserves that would have been offered by the substitution account that has had to be set aside for the time being. Briefly put, these are the ways that the Fund, in exercising its influence on the management of exchange rates and reserves, has been and is being affected by the diffusion of power and the concentration of surpluses.

Discussion

Question: It appears that the most important issue is whether the current or alternative international monetary systems have any effect on the allocation of output between consumption and investment. However, the different views expressed here do not address themselves to the issue. If not, then the only real difference between the different proposals deals with their wealth and income distribution effects, and how does one go about choosing them.

Answer: You cannot compare a flexible-rate system today with a fixed-rate system earlier. You have to ask yourself what sort of system is appropriate to the kinds of political realities that you confront, and the economic realities in the two circumstances. Money probably does not matter that much in the long run for the real side of the economy. However, money and international monetary relations do matter for the conduct of amicable relations between countries and, therefore, for the manner in which they conduct their trade and other economic policies.

To illustrate this, the United States for a long time argued that the value of the dollar was not a matter of grave concern, and we were not trying to protect its value. We called it benign neglect; other people called it other things. The fact is that the value of the dollar did matter to other countries, and they reacted to our policy. This impinged upon our relations with our allies in important economic and political dimensions.

In one sense one has to judge the present regime as being reasonably successful. It has accommodated differences in viewpoints about economic policy, and it has probably promoted economic efficiency because countries have had less incentive to resort to inefficient trade and domestic economic restrictions than they might have had otherwise.

Question: Only glancing references have been made to the role of gold in the reserve system. Would the panel care to comment on how they perceive any residual role for gold in the coming years?

Answer 2: Gold is now being to a large extent remonetized. For example, consider the events of the EMS, where gold is pooled together to some extent, and issues are given against gold. Also, one is seeing that the value of gold is quite important in assessing a country's creditworthiness and ability to borrow. This is particularly important in the case of the European community. Germany's reserves, including gold at market prices, are approaching $100 billion. One does not often see these gold values put formally into a calculation, but everyone knows that it is there. However, I do not think that it is feasible to consider that one could bring back the gold-exchange standard again.

Answer 2: I know that various members of the Fund realized that gold is a pretty valuable asset, and they have varying ideas as to what might be done with it in present circumstances. Furthermore, should the occasion arise for the Fund to borrow, as I think it will, I imagine that those who are contemplating lending to it will recognize that it still has some gold left and will count that among its blessings.

Question: Are there any solutions to the international monetary system other than just telling the national monetary authorities to stay out of the markets? It gets back to an earlier question of whether the best policy might not be no policy as far as foreign-exchange management is concerned. If this were done, then the authorities could concentrate on the recycling problem.

Answer 1: I think you have attributed to me a point of view that I do not share. I spoke to the logic of the speaker, but I did not take a view as to whether intervention was a good or a bad thing.

Answer 2: One of the dimensions that continues to irritate people is that the international system is extraordinarily untidy, disorderly in its structure. I fear that some of the proposals that have come forward are designed not to solve the problems, but rather to make the system neater or tidier. I am not sure that is really a desirable objective. It is an academic objective and may, in fact, explain why academics propose some of the silly things they do propose. We like orderly things because they are easier to explain to our students. This reflects no limitations upon the students' capacity to understand. Rather, it is a limitation upon our capacity to expound.

As for the point that the authorities ought to stay away from the exchange markets, or at least preannounce their targets, may I suggest that there is a contradiction here. If the authorities are prone to muck things up in the exchange markets, who would want to unleash their energies in the solution to the recycling problem? Would they not muck that one up also?

I have some difficulty with the underlying premise that the markets always know better than the authorities, and even more, with the premise that the function of policy is to be predictable in order to make things easier for the private sector. Perhaps a certain element of uncertainty may be essential for the functioning of some of these markets, especially the exchange markets; an element of unpredictability as to what the authorities may do may introduce the sort of friction into the market that is necessary for a degree of stability. Even larger instabilities in the absence of uncertainty may result.

Official intervention has been useful; it has tended to smooth markets; in its absence we might have had wider swings in rates. Of course, intervention unsupported by monetary policies is, over the longer run, futile. Finally, a reform of the reserve system is a high priority issue, but it may be a second-order issue. The issue of maintaining the capacity of developing countries to consume and to invest over the next several years may have a much higher priority than reform of the reserve system per se.

Question: To what extent might any need for international monetary reform be eliminated if central banks in the industrialized countries would pursue less erratic monetary policies during the 1980s?

Answer: Clearly, it is more desirable if countries pursue responsible monetary and fiscal policies. However, even if they all did, countries would still have exchange-rate movements because of exogenous shifts, changes in productivity, and everything else that is going on.

Question: Why is the diversification of assets nearly complete or perhaps complete today? Second to what extent has that diversification affected exchange rates over the last several years?

Answer: The suggestion that the process of diversification may be nearly complete is based on work done at Princeton University. The numbers concerning the dollar's share in central banks' portfolios are coming down into the range of 32–63 percent suggested in that paper. The dollar is now (November 1980) probably under 70 percent, and this share in reserve portfolios is within the range that the central banks want. But this is not a forecast. Only God knows what will happen, or He may not! In fact, it would not be surprising to see the process of diversification away from the dollar go a bit further.

As to the effect on the exchange market, a point another panelist made is worth reiterating: that the trade and financial flows across that market are enormous. Therefore, it is hardly believable that the diversification of official portfolios has been the dominant or the major element in exchange-rate movements over time, but it may have contributed to the weakness of the dollar over the longer period.

14 Financial and Monetary Stability in the 1980s

Robert Triffin

During the 1980 U.S. presidential campaign, the international monetary system was not one of the major issues debated by the candidates. It is even quite possible that they understood relatively little about it, making this campaign little different from those of the last four presidents. President Carter, like Presidents Ford, Nixon, and Johnson before him had a hard time solving the problem. Obviously, none of them did it. The last president who really understood and tried to do something about it was President Kennedy, but even he and then British Prime Minister Harold MacMillan— who shared the same views—were unable to overcome the routine resistance of the bureaucracy and to solve the political problem, which is really a very difficult one: how can one abdicate the "extravagant privilege" of being able to run deficits and pay for them with one's own IOUs?

This has always been very difficult and proved very difficult, as is well known, for President Johnson during the Vietnam war. This so called extravagant privilege is in fact most damaging. It gives us more rope with which to hang ourselves. Let us hope that the longer run view of the problem will be taken by the new administration. If it is not, unfortunately, it may be imposed upon it from the outside. As Peter Kenen points out in chapter 11, it takes two to make the dollar acceptable as a world currency.

The first shortcoming of the system is illustrated by the problem of inflation. It should be stressed that in the last ten years world reserves measured in dollars have increased more than ten times. That means more than ten times the increase of reserves in all previous years and centuries since Adam and Eve, and this surely has something to do with inflation.

What follows is a ranking of the sources of these increasing world reserves in decreasing order of desirability, acceptability, and control by the monetary authorities. The first source, of course, and the only one that reflects an attempt at real international control of the system is the allocations of SDRs and the lending operations of the IMF. But this source, which is the most under control, contributed, according to my calculations, less than 2 percent of the world reserve increases in the last ten years, and less than half of 1 percent last year. The second source of reserve increases is the accumulation of gold by central banks, but the accumulation of gold by central banks in physical terms (at $35 an ounce) has gone down slightly over the last ten years. So it is not responsible for the multiplication of reserves by a factor of ten.

The third source is the accumulation of foreign exchange, particularly dollars, by central banks, and this was the major factor in the 1960s. In the 1960s it explained about 75 percent of the increase in world reserves, but even that has declined in the 1970s to about 25 percent, and last year I believe to about 6 percent. The fourth source of increase is the change in the price of gold and of foreign-exchange rates vis-à-vis the dollar. That explains 73 percent of the increase of world reserves in the last ten years and 93 percent last year alone.

This enumeration of those four sources of reserve increase clearly demonstrates that the authorities have lost control over the system; they could not have lost control more thoroughly than they have. Remember that in 1965, when the governors of central banks and ministers of finance finally decided, belatedly, that something had to be done to reform the international monetary system, they repeatedly stressed the fact that they would review every aspect of the functioning of the international monetary system except two; on those two points there was general agreement that discussion was not necessary because everybody agreed on the two unshakeable features of the world monetary system: stable exchange rates and a stable price of gold, *at $35 an ounce*. That would remain forever.

These are, of course, the two major changes that have occurred in the international monetary system over the last ten years, and I do not know what we have to deplore more: is it the mismanagement that the power to control the system has created, or is it the inability to manage? The second will be with us still for some time to come.

The second major shortcoming is the distribution of reserve investments other than gold. Each year pious resolutions are voted in the United Nations that the capitalized countries should help the financing of the undercapitalized countries. (I prefer the term undercapitalized countries to the euphemism of developing countries in that respect.) It seems reasonable indeed that the richer, more industrialized more capitalized countries should export capital to the less capitalized countries.

But is it not a bit surprising to know that in the area that is, or should be most under the control of the monetary and political authorities, that is, the international monetary system, exactly the opposite has been done? Of the increase in international reserves other than gold over the last ten years, about 4 percent went to the poorer, least capitalized countries, and 96 percent to the richer, industrial countries. This is bound to create more and more problems and, of course, is discussed by the Brandt Commission.

What has been the reaction of the economists and of responsible political and monetary leaders to this extraordinary collapse of the system? I would hazard the rough guess that 90 percent of the economic papers and books I have read recently—excepting, of course, by Peter Kenen—have essentially devoted their time to discussing the relative merits and demerits

of stable- versus flexible-exchange rates. It is an important subject undoubtedly, but as long as the reserve system can be flooded, as it has been in
the past, by the so-called reserve currencies of one or a few deficit countries,
neither fixed- nor flexible-exchange rates can function satisfactorily.

Another reason for the problem, of course, which has been stressed by
all, is the explosion of oil prices at the end of 1973. Undoubtedly, this has
contributed enormously to our problem—this cannot be denied. But do not
forget that it happened at the end of 1973, two years after the collapse of
Bretton Woods and of the convertibility of the dollar, and years after the
start of inflation.

World reserves had already doubled, increasing just as much as since
Adam and Eve, in the years 1970-1972, well before the explosion of oil
prices, which was in part at least a consequence of, and a reaction to, this
inflationary phenomenon.

This should be sufficient demonstration of the need to go back to the
problem of international monetary reform—and not simply to the Triffin
Plan of 1959—but to the last report on this subject by the directors of the
International Monetary Fund and to the swan song of the Committee of
Twenty in June 1974. I regret very much, of course, that all this on which
some degree of international consensus seemed to be emerging was buried
or at least put on ice—I do not know for how long—in Jamaica, and in the
Second Amendment to the International Monetary Fund agreement, which
I would simply describe or characterize as a sinister joke.

It was simply legalizing, after many years, the illegality that had resulted
from the repudiation of the Bretton Woods commitments by most countries, without any serious agreement yet as to what could be put in their
place. There is still a long chapter, of course, on "obligations of members
regarding exchange arrangements," but outside of some jargon it can be
summarized in the end in one word or in one sentence of that article. It says
that any country can adopt whatever exchange arrangements it wishes, except only the one to which they all had been committed before, that is, to
denominate their currency in terms of gold. The only thing that was permitted
before is now banned, but outside of that a country can do what it wishes. A
country can fix its currency in terms of dollars, sterling, the French franc, or
the various and different batches of different currencies. There is not even a
common measure for the exchange rates under the present system!

A return is needed to the proposals on which people had finally agreed
after years of negotiations. Of course, more problems have emerged since
then. In chapter 12 David Lomax discusses the importance of the role of the
private banks. Certainly there is a lot that has developed in terms of the
financing of the international disequilibria by the private market, which is
far more important than anything that the Fund is doing or that even central banks are doing. That certainly deserves a look.

Another new factor is the extraordinary developments in the gold market. Little has been said about gold in this volume, but gold prices and changes in gold prices are obviously one of the major factors—not yet in the present inflation—in the possibility of further inflation later on.

For instance, take one simple example: The issue of ECUs in Europe in one year and a half has increased by about 74 percent, but not because of excessive credits to members; credits to members were zero. All of it came from increases in the price of gold. This, of course, produces enormous bookkeeping profits for the central banks, and the way in which this phenomenon of bookkeeping profits is dealt with under present arrangements is the exact counterpart of common sense.

If a country is forced to devalue its currency because it has followed too expansionist or inflationary policies, the central bank accumulates enormous profits, and sooner or later these profits are passed on to the government and the treasury, facilitating more expenditures, possibly leading again to more deficits, more devaluation, and more profits in an endless and vicious cycle.

Exactly the opposite phenomenon is possible—which may be relevant in forthcoming months. If a currency appreciates, the central banks suffer losses, and there are many arguments that they should tighten their policies, leading to further surpluses, further appreciation, and further bookkeeping losses ad nauseam.

All this will, one hopes, reduce some radical changes—contrary, again, to the opinion of most of the other book contributors—but I suspect that even the most optimistic view is that those changes in the world monetary system will still take some time to negotiate. The result of this is that the major moves that can be contemplated, in the immediate future at least, will come from regional monetary cooperation. Let us hope that far more attention will be paid by politicians, private bankers, and academic economists to a phenomenon they have not sufficiently discussed, namely, the implications of the attempt to create more regional monetary agreement, first as a sort of oasis in a chaotic world monetary system or non-system and, second, as a way to put more pressure on major countries—particularly the United States—to participate in meaningful international monetary reform and to try to help the transition.

Those arrangements, properly conducted, could help strengthen the dollar and make return to a more sensible monetary system more feasible.[1]

The changes that have occurred in Europe, particularly the creation of the European Monetary System, can at least achieve two objectives. The first, for which we have pleaded for a long time, is to decrease interventions in dollars on the European exchange markets. When the situation among foreign countries changes, even if nothing has happened in the United States, there may be a boost to the dollar or further bearish speculation on the dollar, depending on who accumulates reserves.

In early 1977 Italy and Britain, for instance, were delighted to take up more dollars, but when their position changed and the surpluses corresponding to U.S. deficits went to Germany and Switzerland, these countries were much less willing to absorb them. Suddenly, there was a big turnaround in the dollar market, even though nothing substantial had changed in U.S. policies. This may change if, as hoped for, there are alternatives to dollar financing of international disequilibrium, but this has not been achieved yet. It must be stressed that of the enormous interventions on the exchange markets today in Europe only a small fraction go through the EMS. The only interventions going through the EMS are those that take place at the margins, that is, when a currency reaches its ceiling or its floor, but the bulk of intervention still takes place intramarginally and is conducted very much as it was before, that is to say, in dollars.

The second contribution that the EMS could make is to help in the financing of the tapering-off deficits of the United States. The ECU might be used for substitution accounts, as well as the SDR. Some nations might be reluctant to accumulate SDRs but be willing to accumulate ECUs. Let us have no exclusive attachment to one system rather than another in that respect. From that point of view, of course, some progress has been made in the United States with the willingness to intervene in the market, with the willingness to borrow not only from central banks but from the market itself, with the willingness to denominate some of that indebtedness in marks or yen, and so on, rather than only in dollars.

If some of those borrowings could be dominated in ECUs rather than in marks, this would be politically more attractive. It would be a demonstration of the willingness of the U.S. administration to cooperate with Europeans, rather than giving the appearance that the dollar has become a satellite of the mark. I think this political consideration might have some impact on the Congress and the Administration.

I cannot develop in detail here my view that the European Fund for Monetary Cooperation could accumulate some of its investments in the United States in the formerly prestigious form of *consols*, that is, obligations without any fixed repayment date. This would indeed adjust the international financing system to the facts of life. Regardless of one's preference, it is impossible for a country in deficit to repay its indebtedness. As long as it remains in deficit, it will accumulate more indebtedness.

The same thing is true for the countries in surplus. As long as a country remains in surplus it cannot be repaid in real terms. It will accumulate more claims abroad. But this is disguised by the way in which our international contracts are written; they sometimes induce improper policies.

Those are the views I am trying to push as much as possible not only in the European Community, but also in the OPEC countries and the nonoil-exporting LDC countries. The development of regional monetary cooperation is not simply an unavoidable transition toward the restoration of a worldwide system, but it should be part and parcel of ultimate international monetary reforms.

The International Monetary Fund should be very much decentralized, and if some problems can be solved on a regional basis there is no need to run to Washington each time to involve the scarce time of the Fund in problems that can be solved regionally. Moreover, this would help make the Fund's operations more acceptable to countries that are now totally outside, or to the countries that have been complaining about Fund policies, particularly some of the less-developed countries.

If a less-developed country in deficit should first have to turn to its peers and seek financing or help from a regional organization, the conditions put on such help would probably be more realistic, taking into view the account of the less-developed countries themselves. But there would still be conditions, and if these conditions are not accepted the IMF could not be blamed for trying to impose the views of industrial countries upon the less-developed countries.

This might also help in the other problem that is very much discussed today, the problem of voting power. Whatever changes are made in voting power, it is obvious that no group can get an absolute majority. Every group will always be in a minority, and at least each group can deal itself with its own internal problems; that would diffuse the issue to some extent.

Note

1. R. Triffin, "The Future of the International Monetary System," *Banca Nazionale del Lavoro Quarterly Review,* no. 132 (March 1980), pp. 29-55.

Discussion

Question: Has the big increase in international reserves in the last decade contributed to volatility or to stability?

Answer: To answer briefly, to volatility certainly. But some people have suggested that the enormous increase in reserves is due, in part, to the views of the disciples of Triffin—that there was a reserve shortage. I never said that! I said in 1959 that there was a dilemma; that either we would restore equilibrium and find a substitute for the dollar, or the U.S. deficit would continue and there would be growth in the dollar crisis.

A look at the figures will show that the increase in the allocations of SDRs have been a totally insignificant portion of the total increase in reserves. In fact, the gentleman who made the complaint about Triffin's disciples was at that time accumulating billions and billions of dollars in his central bank, and that had much more to do with the problem than the SDR.

Question: You seem to equate increases in reserves due to paper profits and capital gains with increases in reserves due to interventions by the central banks. Would you agree that they have the same inflationary consequences? It would seem at least that they have come through different channels.

Answer: Obviously, the bookkeeping profits of central banks have not yet increased actual money supplies or inflation. The central banks value gold very largely at $35 or $42 an ounce. Those profits have not been passed out yet to the public in actual circulation. What I was stressing is the fact that sooner or later such profits are always passed on to the treasuries. The central banks try to postpone that evil day as long as they can, but in the end they do so, and at that time the fictitious cycle I was describing before may occur.

Question: Is there anything that can be done to prevent the tremendous appreciation in gold values from being monetized? In other words, can we somehow avoid the inflationary consequences of the potentially massive increases in base money that will occur if and when central banks begin to value gold at market values instead of at $35 or $42 an ounce?

Answer: What I am trying to promote in Europe at the moment are some sort of guidelines on what can be done with those big bookkeeping profits, and I think the solution is fairly simple economically, although maybe very difficult politically. It is simply that all profits or losses on foreign reserves will be passed on to a devaluation account in which profits and losses can be offset against one another, but none are passed on to the treasury; those are blocked accounts. Of course, various qualifications or exceptions can be made. For instance, instead of making another loan to a country, it could be allowed to use its gold profits.

Question: What are your views about a multiple-reserve-currency system, as the world is now evolving toward, versus a system with one dominate international asset such as the SDR?

Answer: I am not in favor of multiple-currency reserves, but as long as there are still reserve currencies—the dollar, the deutsche mark, and so forth—in existence, then something like the ECU might help to introduce some kind of order in the system. However, I would like to emphasize that, in the longer run, I do not conceive that the ECU should be a substitute for SDRs. In fact, I have been pointing out repeatedly that Europe should not push the ECU; this proved so disastrous for sterling in September 1931 and for the dollar nearly forty years later in August 1971. Of course, any composite currency or international asset such as the SDR is difficult to introduce to the public and to manage. However, the use of national currencies as international reserves is bound to be more inflationary; the only way to have a system that is not excessively inflationary is to be able to control the quantity of the international reserve asset.

Question: You seem to say that if we move from national currencies as international reserves to an international asset as international reserves, the inflation problem would somehow be solved. I do not quite understand how that would work.

Answer: I would not say it would solve the inflation problem in each individual country. However, at least insofar as international contracts are concerned, a system is needed that does not subject the borrower or the lender to excessive windfall losses or profits. This can be achieved if international loans are denominated in an international asset such as the SDR. On the whole some amount of stability there would be more desirable, and this might have something to do with the recovery of worldwide economic activity. It is not a panacea, but it is important. I am concerned with unemployment as well as with inflation, but if I have to choose between the two, I would choose inflation rather than unemployment. However, the events of the last few years have demonstrated that inflation is not a remedy for recession and unemployment. It may spur new problems of recession. In sum, to recover the chances for an economic climate conducive to recovery and lowering unemployment some arresting of the present wave of inflation is an absolute prerequisite.

Question: Does not your proposal require a very dramatic, albeit gradual, change in the whole functioning of the international market and indeed the introduction of the SDR as the vehicle for virtually all international financial transactions?

Answer: We certainly have to think and to innovate with respect to a radical view of the possible or necessary reform in the whole system of international lending, private as well as public. But the SDR would not be the only solution. Insofar as central banks accumulating reserves, it might be reasonable to make the SDR the main instrument or maybe even the exclusive instrument, except for minor working balances of foreign exchange. I would also give private banks access to the SDR. Outside of that, there would be other forms of international investment. I would be very willing to look at Bob Roosa's proposals, for instance, to provide also some kind of investment instrument that would be acceptable outside the SDR.

Part V
Meeting Developing Countries' Financial Needs in the 1980s

Corrado Pirzio-Biroli

There has been much talk about reserve and exchange-rate management. The financing of the nonoil developing countries' needs in the 1980s is the major subject of this section. In fact, the debate on the future of the SDR and notably the substitution account has been put on the back burner to some extent by putting the resource-transfer problem at the center of the stage. I think a few figures are illustrative in showing the plight of the nonoil developing countries. In 1973-1979 they suffered an average terms of trade loss of 1-1.5 percent per annum, which is equal to a cumulative loss of $80 billion, mostly because of inflated exports from advanced industrialized countries, and also, to some extent, because of increased oil prices. Although oil represents only about one-fifth of their total imports on average, they will be paying almost twice as much for oil this year as they receive in foreign aid. Overseas Development Assistance paid about one-quarter of the current-account deficits before transfers for 1979.

The optimists say that there is no reason to worry, that the world's balance of payments must balance. Deficits must be matched by surpluses. Current-account imbalances exist only if they are financed. They say that in real terms the recycling problem is not much more serious than in 1974-1975. The optimists also say that the commercial banks will do whatever is left over from the international financial institutions and bilateral organizations. Finally, they say that oil prices cannot be sustained for very long.

The pessimists retort that advanced industrialized countries will try to go quickly back into balance, not excluding capital-export restraints, leaving all the deficits to the less-developed countries. They say that major-borrowing developing countries are unlikely to hold up their growth rates as they did in 1974-1975. They maintain that commercial banks will be reluctant to finance persistent external deficits because of higher exposure and loan concentration, portfolio limits, lower yields, and higher risks.

It appears that the next couple of years will be a critical period. Henry Kaufman said that the recycling problem is like a time bomb ticking away at the international monetary system. This time we cannot hope that OPEC will bail us out by letting real oil prices go down, which is what happened last time.

131

15 Financial Problems of Nonoil Developing Countries

Jacques Polak

The Group of Thirty has established a study group that deals with the same subject this chapter examines—the financial needs of the developing countries in the 1980s. I am a member of that study group and have done a lot of work for it. Its report is some distance from completion and I am pleased to be able to use this discussion to ventilate some of the ideas in the report—not necessarily all my own.

There is no question that the financial problems facing the nonoil developing countries in the 1980s will be very large. The size of the deficit on current account in the balance of payments of these countries has been estimated by the IMF to be about $70 billion this year and possibly on the order of $80 billion next year.

Although this discussion centers primarily on the question of the covering of this deficit, this financing problem is not the most important or the most serious problem of the developing countries. The most serious problem for these countries in the next decade is that their development will have to take place in surroundings that are much less favorable than those of the 1970s, let alone those of the 1960s. There is a severe deterioration in two respects.

First, there is the rise in oil costs or, more generally, the worsening of their terms of trade. These countries will have to use, roughly speaking, twice as much of their own production to pay for their imports of oil. Second, there is the flattening of demand in the industrial world. The industrial countries will inevitably grow much more slowly in the 1980s than in the two preceding decades. For the LDCs this will mean a much less buoyant demand for their primary products, much less prosperous markets in which to sell their industrial products, and also much greater risks of protectionism.

These two negative factors will inevitably put a damper on the speed of development in the LDC world. It would be out of the question for these countries to maintain their previous rates of growth by borrowing more even if creditors existed that were prepared to lend the enormous amounts that would be involved. All that such an approach would do would be to replace a difficult present situation by an impossible future situation—and not far in the future either.

On the contrary, only as LDCs adjust their economies to the new surroundings will they be sufficiently credit-worthy to attract needed capital flows. That applies to official as well as to private flows. Creditworthiness in this context is not some outrageous condiion imposed by the World Bank or the commercial banks or the Fund. The countries themselves in surveying their future would come to the same conclusion, and, of course, most of them have come to that conclusion.

Only countries that adjust can expect to be living in the future on a rising trend of output, and only a rising trend of output can provide a rational basis for borrowing, that is, for the assumption that the future will be sufficiently better than the present to make it sensible to borrow now and repay later.

The previously mentioned current-account deficit for the nonoil LDCs in the early 1980s—$70–$80 billion—is about twice as high as the deficits of the same countries in the mid-1970s. We should not be too intimidated by large numbers, what one of my colleagues in the Group of Thirty calls "Megalophobia."

Since the mid-1970s the economies of the LDCs have been growing substantially at the rate of roughly 5 percent per year and, of course, inflation has raised world prices so that the new numbers—about twice as high as the older numbers—are in fact somewhat lower as a percentage of GDP than the numbers in the 1970s. Of these numbers in the 1970s the Fund pointed out some years ago that they were not really higher in real comparable terms than the amount of capital that developing countries had been absorbing in the late 1960s and before the oil shortage in the 1970s.

One has to say at the same time that there is a clear deterioration in another dimension, namely, that unlike the experience after the first oil shock these deficits are likely to persist on a large scale at least to the middle of the decade.

When we discuss the financing problem of the nonoil LDCs we tend to focus attention on the countries that have access to credits from the commercial banks. Indeed, there is perhaps too much of a tendency to see this problem entirely as a commercial bank-major LDC problem. Actually these countries are small in number, perhaps some twenty, and those are the ones that have the advantage either that they export some oil—such as, for example, Mexico, Peru, and Syria—or that they are exporters of industrial products, such as Brazil, Argentina, Korea, Israel and Yugoslavia, all countries that are classified by the IMF in this large group of nonoil-exporting LDCs.

The twenty countries in these two groups account for half the deficit of the nonoil LDCs and for three-quarters of their total borrowing, but they are only a small number of countries and most of them are among the most fortunate of the developing countries in many respects. The poorest developing countries simply are not in a position to have recourse to private credit to meet their payments difficulties. These are not the countries that make the headlines of crises of overborrowing, followed by massive rescue operations. What is needed for these countries is more adequate concessional aid, both multilateral and bilateral, and all the help that the Fund can give them.

Quantitatively, too, aid is one important component in the flow of finance to developing countries that should be set against the $70–$80 billion figure. Also, direct investment is important. To mention another component, there is very great need for much increased flows from the oil-surplus countries directly to the LDCs, not through the financial institutions in the industrial countries.

When all is said and done on these various aspects it will remain true that, as in the 1970s, the principal channel of intermediation for the more fortunate LDCs will have to be through the commercial banks. Much has been made of the difficulties to which the commercial banks would be subject in continuing to perform this function. I would agree, however, with the tenor of a recent speech by the managing director of the Fund that these difficulties can be overcome and that the commercial banks will again play the major role in the recycling process. However, this role must be backstopped by the IMF, an IMF that is strong enough to perform its task fully.

This will require the availability to the IMF and most likely also the use by the IMF of resources on an unprecedented scale. Only if the Fund can offer finance on a substantial scale to a country in difficult circumstances can it effectively encourage the adoption of constructive policy changes. Moreover, the risks are not exclusively with the policies of individual countries. The risk also exists that important links in the recycling mechanism may break down, with possibly wider consequences, and in such circumstances the Fund must be ready to support the solidity of the system as a whole.

The case for a larger role by the Fund does not rest, of course, on calculations of a huge gap between the likely scale of private flows and the needs of developing countries in general. If the system runs smoothly, thanks in part to the Fund's action in individual cases, such a gap may never arise; but the Fund's operations with individual countries, in particular if some of these countries are very large countries, will involve very sizeable amounts in any event. This is one of the reasons why it would not be wise for the Fund to fritter away such resources as it will be able to obtain in across-the-board intermediation for its own sake.

The resources that the Fund can use can essentially come from two sources: quota contributions and borrowing. Unfortunately, quota increases in the Fund have not kept pace with the growth of international transactions, and even less with the growth of international imbalances. Even after the current increase will have gone into effect aggregate quotas will amount to only 4 percent of the imports of members as against 10 percent in 1970 and even somewhat higher percentages in the 1960s.

There is simply no question, therefore, that the Fund will have to take recourse to borrowing if it is to provide its members with assistance on a scale commensurate with the size of the problems that these members are likely to encounter in present circumstances. These borrowings may be obtained, as they were in the past, from surplus countries, in particular the oil-surplus countries, or the Fund might tap the capital market. It can perform its economic recycling role in either of two ways. Direct borrowing from oil exporters would be advantageous if this could be done at low cost, which may not be all that likely. Otherwise, there would be advantages in the anonymity and the flexibility of using the market. The best solution is likely to consist in a judicious combination of the two sources.

Borrowed money will be expensive money. However, for countries whose alternative source of finance would be the Euromarkets even borrowed Fund money would still come somewhat cheaper than market resources, on the assumption that the credit rating of the Fund in the market, which has not yet been established, will be better than anybody else's. But for low-income developing countries borrowed money passed on by the Fund will simply be too expensive. In recognition of this fact, the Fund has recently established a subsidy account to bring down the effect of interest-rate costs.

Given the international backing and the assets that the Fund commands, there can be little doubt that the problems of resources for the Fund can be overcome. It is not necessary, to elaborate any more on this particular problem. The far more difficult issue before the Fund is on the other side of its transactions, namely, for the Fund to find the conditions for its lending activities that will meet the twin tests for its success.

These tests are: (1) that countries in need of adjustment action will come to the Fund for its assitance; (2) that the nature, intensity, and speed of adjustment on which the Fund will insist will be sufficient to restore over time the economic and financial viability of the countries that draw its resources.

One has to realize that in this respect the Fund is faced with a clear dilemma. If its conditions are too rigorous, countries may have recourse to highly undesirable restrictive policies as long as they possibly can in order to stay out of the Fund. But if the conditions imposed by the Fund are too loose, the Fund's resources may simply be poured into situations that fail to be remedied. The credit-worthiness of the countries will not be restored; the countries will not regain access to market flows of capital; and the credit extended by the Fund may in fact turn out to be frozen.

An interesting question in this connection—that was discussed at considerable length in the subgroup of the Committee of Thirty—was how far the Fund could develop its Article Four Consultations with its members to generate a continuing understanding with each member on the adequacy of its policies. Such an understanding would help to facilitate and thereby compress in time the negotiations that would be required to reach agreement on a standby arrangement in case the need for such an arrangement materialized.

A closer association between the Fund and its members through more intensive use of the consultations procedures would reduce the risk to which the international financing mechanism is exposed, and it would also be likely to improve the adjustment process even if such an association did not lead to a very large volume of Fund transactions.

Although the commercial banks have performed an outstanding recycling job over the past few years, there are certain tasks in the international adjustment process that are simply beyond their reach but that the Fund can perform. First, the Fund is in a position to monitor the performance of members' economies, and it can advise members on this as well as advise the public on it.

Second, in its consultative role in the context of Article Four, the Fund's periodic inquiries into the policies of member countries are likely to act as a desirable constraint even where no specific limits, such as limits on credit, are agreed with a country. And, finally, the Fund's analysis of global economic interrelations is essential both as a background for members' policies and for the effective operation of the Fund itself; and its ability to perform these functions is critically dependent on its thorough understanding of the conditions and the policies of its member countries.

Where countries do require finance there is a very strong case for the Fund to stand ready to provide its assistance on a larger scale than has hitherto been the practice and over a longer period. The kind of adjustment called for by the adverse change in countries' external circumstances, which was previously referred to, will often require structural changes that can bear fruit only over an extended period.

The Fund has already gone a long way in the last few months (of 1980) to modify its practices along these lines. It has adopted a guideline for the amount of assistance it is willing to grant—600 percent of quota over a three-year period, with annual limits of 200 percent of quota, which constitutes a sixfold increase, again in terms of quotas, of the amount of assistance that the Fund used to be ready to have available in normal circumstances until a few years ago. The Fund has also shifted its emphasis from one-year to three-year standby arrangements, and it has lengthened the maximum period of repayment under what is called in the Fund the "extended Fund facility" from eight years to ten years.

All these changes have the effect of mitigating the dilemma for the Fund that was referred to earlier. If a country can obtain assistance from the Fund on a much larger scale, this improves its cost-benefit tradeoff in its decision whether to come to the Fund or not. Increased financing over a longer period makes it possible for a country to reduce the extent of the adjustment necessary in the first year of an arrangement with the Fund, while still committing itself to a course of action that can be expected to achieve the needed adjustment over time.

Because of the nature of the adjustment problems that many countries face in present circumstances, the Fund's approach in the field of adjustment will have to be broader than that on which it placed its main emphasis in the past, which was the correction of inadequate financial policies. Action in this field will still be needed in those cases where such policies, inadequate financial policies, are the major cause of a country's payments difficulties, but other policy changes may be needed in almost all countries that will come to the Fund—that is, policies to adjust the economies of these countries to the two fundamental changes in the economic environment: the slower growth in the industrial countries and the sharp increase in the price of energy. These latter policy changes generally lie in the area of supply of new commodities for export, for example, or of alternative sources of energy, and so on.

To assure itself about the general credit-worthiness of the countries it assists the Fund will need to concern itself with supply policies, not in substitution for but in addition to its concern with demand policies. It is obvious that in dealing with policies on the supply side the Fund approaches the area of competence of the World Bank, just as the World Bank is approaching the Fund's field of activity by extending its lending activities to what it calls structural-financing needs. These convergent changes in the activities of the two institutions call for close collaboration between them, and there are welcome signs of movement in this direction.

As is well known, the Bank's financial activities consist primarily in making project loans but also to a smaller extent in giving balance-of-payments credit. The most interesting development on the project side in the Bank is its plan to create a new energy affiliate that would permit it to expand its lending program in the energy field to a figure of $25 billion over a five-year period. Such a program would contribute directly to a reduction of world energy imbalances and strike at a root cause of the recycling problem. It would also provide relief on a very important scale to the current account of the developing countries by the year 1990.

In order to assist developing countries in dealing constructively with their immediate payments problems the Bank has recently adopted a policy of granting what are called structural-adjustment loans. Such loans are intended to help countries to ride out present difficulties in the world situation and to make the adjustments in their policies to meet these changes in the world situation, and these loans are intended as being complementary to the adjustment assistance provided by the IMF.

One has to bear in mind that in general the Bank and its subsidiaries are to a far greater extent than the Fund subject to constraints on the amount of resources they can make available. To mention one example, International Development Association (IDA) commitments have been delayed by the slowness of IDA ratification. Also, the rate of lending by the World Bank for project and other purposes combined is kept down by statutory provisions of the Bank and also by the views of major member countries on the proper volume of the Bank's activities.

These limits on lending by the Bank family mean that the main emphasis in official recycling for the first half of this decade will have to fall on the IMF, but the largest part of total recycling will again have to be performed by the private-capital markets, supported in their function by a much strengthened IMF.

16 Financial Needs of the Developing Countries in the 1980s

Alvin J. Karchere

The international agencies assume very modest increases in the price of crude oil when making balance-of-payments and other projections. As an example, the IMF in its May 1980 *World Economic Outlook* assumes that the real price of oil will remain unchanged through 1981. Similarly, the World Bank in its *World Development Report 1980* assumes that real oil prices will rise by 3 percent a year through 1990. Changes in these assumptions make major differences in the balance-of-payments situations of the developing countries, their ability to finance their deficits, and, therefore, their ability to sustain a reasonable rate of growth.

As an aid to understanding the likely movement of crude-oil prices in the future, the events in the crude-oil market that followed the Iranian revolution make an interesting case study. In October 1978 Iran was producing 5.5 million barrels per day (MBD) of crude oil; in January 1979 that had fallen to 0.5 MBD; by January 1980 Iranian production had only increased to 2.3 MBD. Despite the loss of Iranian production OPEC produced more crude in 1979 than in 1978. This was accomplished because the members of OPEC, excluding Iran, raised their operating rates to 95 percent of maximum sustainable capacity. In these circumstances the price of crude oil increased rapidly in the Rotterdam spot market and the contract prices of members of OPEC followed not far behind the spot market. The 75 percent increase in the price of crude oil in 1979 was the result of market forces that OPEC countries followed. It was not caused by a concerted OPEC decision.

A survey of informed opinion on the balance of supply and demand for crude oil over the next decade yields uniform conclusions. For example, the International Energy Agency in its report on 1979 policies and programs concludes that there will be a shortfall of supply in the 1980s. The Congressional Budget Office's recent report on the world oil market comes to the same conclusion. The forecast shortfall is an indication of a very tight supply-demand situation. Of course there will not be a supply deficit; demand and supply will be brought into balance by rising prices.

In the Congressional Budget Office forecast demand is growing very slowly. However, supply originating in OPEC and the industrial countries is increasing hardly at all, and the Soviet bloc is changing from a small net

The views expressed are those of the author, not those of IBM.

exporter of oil to a small net importer. The growth in supply is taking place in the nonOPEC LDCs, at a 7.5 percent annual rate, but that increase is from a small base. The International Energy Agency also forecasts only a small increase in supply. The recent study of the Office of Technology Assessment of the U.S. Congress on *World Petroleum Availability 1980-2000* also concludes that during the next two decades "it is highly likely that there will be little or no increase in world production of oil from conventional sources."

If the projections of very tight oil supply in the 1980s are correct, and there seems little reason to doubt that they are, they have implications for the future price of crude oil. These projections imply that in periods of economic expansion OPEC capacity utilization will be at the 95 percent level. In effect, the supply of oil will be the limiting factor on world economic expansion, and the world economy will move from periods of expansion and excess demand for oil to periods of contraction and stagnation when oil will be in excess supply.

We can expect a large increase in oil prices when OPEC is operating at 95 percent of capacity. This will happen even if Saudi Arabia and its supporters in OPEC try to moderate the size of the price increases. In periods of weak demand Saudi Arabia has great influence in OPEC because, without harm to itself, Saudi Arabia can cut back on production and thus stabilize the price of oil. When Saudi Arabia is operating at full capacity, and there is excess demand, it is unable to exert a moderating influence.

The difference in views on oil prices between Saudi Arabia and such price hawks as Algeria or Nigeria is founded on economic interest and is, therefore, fundamental. Saudi Arabian reserves are almost fifty times current production, whereas they are only about twenty times for Algeria and Nigeria; moreover, Algeria and Nigeria have large populations relative to their oil income. They wish, therefore, to get high prices from current production. The Saudi Arabians can afford to be more relaxed about current prices because their current oil revenues are in excess of their current needs and they expect to get high prices from their ample reserves in the future.

Apart from economic arguments, the political instability of the area suggests that it is probable that there will be another, or more than one, substantial supply interruption during the 1980s. The present conflict between Iraq and Iran fortuitously has taken place at a time when the world is in recession—a direct result of the oil price increases that were caused by the Iranian revolution. The war between Iraq and Iran started at a time when stocks were ample and production of oil was in excess of demand. Nevertheless, the spot price of oil has already moved from $30 to $40 a barrel.

There is no doubt that if the war between Iran and Iraq continues for another six months, and if the crude oil terminals and pipeline pumping stations are substantially damaged and take a long time to repair, we will see another round of large price increases for crude oil. If the increases are half as great as those that followed the Iranian revolution, the price of crude could be $55 a barrel by the end of 1982.

In a more favorable scenario the war ends in the next several months and, within three or four months after that, crude exports from Iraq and Iran are restored to 4 MBD. In that scenario the world would have lost about six months exports from Iraq and Iran, about 2 MBD. There would be some increase in the price of crude in 1981, perhaps $5 or $6 a barrel, raising it to about $37 a barrel in 1981. In addition the reduction in inventories would hasten the day of 95 percent capacity utilization and rapidly rising crude prices in the next expansion.

There are two reasons to think that it may be possible to limit the increases in the real price of crude over the next decade to 3 percent or so. First, over the long run the price of crude oil can not exceed the price of synthetic crude oil made from coal. Estimates indicate that synthetic crude will be produced at about $45 a barrel in 1980 prices. But that has significance only if demand and supply of oil are in long-run equilibrium, which implies substantial production of synthetic crude for use as transportation fuel and a shift off oil on to other fuels for industrial heating and steam raising. We will have to wait for that circumstance at least until the 1990s. In the meantime, the cost of synthetic crude will have little influence on OPEC prices.

The second reason for a possible moderation in oil prices is an OPEC self-imposed limitation. The moderates in OPEC under the leadership of Saudi Arabia have been trying to get agreement to a long-term pricing policy, so far without success. In view of the difference in economic interests between those members of OPEC that have large reserves and small populations and those that have small reserves and large populations, the prospects for agreement seem very poor. And even if an agreement could be reached it is doubtful that it would stand the strain of a very tight market in which spot prices were rising rapidly. Neither an OPEC agreement nor the price of synthetic crude will be an effective limit on the price of crude oil in the 1980s.

If the average OPEC crude oil price is $37 a barrel in 1981, the average annual rate of increase from 1973 will be 38 percent. That includes two episodes of rapid and large price increases. If we consider the period 1973 to 1978, so as to exclude the crude price increases associated with the Iranian revolution, the increase is 36 percent.

Given what we know about the balance of supply and demand for crude oil, the unavailability of substitute fuels, the warring economic interests of the OPEC countries, and the political and military instability in the Middle East, the only reason to expect that there will not be continued increases of 36 percent in crude-oil prices over the next five years is that the world financial system would not survive it. Therefore, the consequences of an increase in crude-oil prices of half the 36 percent rate, that is 18 percent a year in nominal prices between now and 1985 will be examined. That level of increase would mean $72 a barrel of oil in 1985.

On the assumption that the OPEC countries that have a balance-of-payments surplus increase their imports at the same rate as in 1977-1979, 25 percent a year in current prices, and that the OPEC deficit countries increase their imports at a rate a little more rapid than their export earnings, the OPEC balance-of-payments surplus will be $150 billion in 1985 and average $125 billion between 1980 and 1985. On average, this amounts to 1.1 percent of the noncommunist world GNP. In 1974, at its high point, the OPEC surplus was 1.3 percent of the noncommunist world GNP, but thereafter it diminished very rapidly. This decrease is not likely in the 1980s because OPEC imports will be rising more slowly and prices more rapidly than in the 1970s. The financing of balance-of-payments deficits, therefore, will be a problem of major proportions in the 1980s for the oil-importing countries. Those countries that are attractive to foreign investors will not have as much difficulty as others that are less fortunate.

The oil-importing developing countries will have the greatest problems. According to the *World Development Report, 1980* of the World Bank, the high-case projections for the oil-importing developing countries produce balance-of-payments financing requirements of $85 billion in 1985, about a $30 billion increase from 1980. It should be noted in passing that the World Bank high case assumes per capita GNP growth for these countries of a little more than 2 percent between 1980 and 1985.

Under the World Bank's assumptions of about a 3 percent increase in the real price of crude oil, the nominal price would rise to $50 a barrel by 1985. If, we assume, the price is $72 a barrel in 1985 rather than $50, and the oil-importing developing countries do not reduce their imports, but do increase their exports to their oil suppliers, and suffer an increase in debt and interest payments, their balance-of-payments deficit will worsen by $38 billion. This changes the balance-of-payments financing requirements for the oil-importing developing countries in the World Bank's high case from barely possible to one of great difficulty. The balance-of-payments financing requirements for those countries in 1985 would be 117 percent higher than 1980, compared with an 85 percent increase in the previous five years. In those circumstances, by 1985 about 50 percent of the oil-importing developing countries' export earnings would be used to pay for their oil imports and interest on their debt, a significant increase from 37 percent in 1980. The oil-importing developing countries will suffer a 3.5 percent a year worsening in their terms of trade caused solely by oil imports.

The increase in oil prices will confront the oil-importing developing countries with a stark dilemma. They can take the consequences of the dramatic shift of the terms of trade against them in the present and accept a reduction in their standard of living. Alternatively, they may try to postpone the reduction in their standard of living by borrowing at market interest rates to finance these additional deficits caused by rising oil prices. The strategy of postponing would be a good one if there were a temporary bulge in the deficit that could be paid in the future when economic growth would make the pain of adjustment easier. If oil prices continue to increase throughout the 1980s at high rates this is not a workable strategy because the balance-of-payments trends present in the first half of the 1980s would accelerate in the second half of the 1980s, and the burden of debt would become intolerable. From the point of view of the oil-importing countries, the only possibilities for ameliorating the effects of the rising oil prices on their standards of living are increased foreign aid or loans at low rates of interest.

How does the situation look through the eyes of private lenders? If they conclude that the OPEC surplus in the 1980s will diminish from a high point in 1980 to a negligible amount in the late 1980s, as it did in the 1970s, and that there will be an improvement in the balance of payments of the oil-importing developing countries, then they will conclude that the oil-importing developing countries are good credit risks. If the private lenders become convinced that the real price of crude oil will grow at rates significantly greater than the 3 percent assumed by the World Bank, they will not be able to escape the conclusion that the oil-importing developing countries are poor credit risks—unless those countries take on the very painful burden of adjustment or obtain major increases in foreign aid or concessionary loans.

The industrial countries in the 1980s will also have great economic problems. Like the developing countries, they will have to cope with deterioration in the terms of trade and current-account deficits. Their adjustment process will be eased by capital inflow from the OPEC countries, but the 1980s will be a period of little improvement in standard of living, high unemployment, and continued high inflation. This is not an atmosphere in which generosity thrives. The prospect of substantial increases in foreign aid from the industrial countries cannot be considered good.

This leaves OPEC. OPEC foreign aid as a percentage of its GNP substantially exceeds that of the industrial countries. Having said this, it is also true that the OPEC surplus is the other side of the oil-importing countries deficits. OPEC will enjoy a huge improvement in terms of trade and could afford a substantial increase in foreign aid for the developing countries. Perhaps it would be possible for them to consider giving, as aid to the developing countries, a fraction of the additional revenue they get when the real price of oil increases by more than 1 or 2 percent a year.

To sum up, the experts have concluded that it is highly likely that there will be little or no increase in the supply of crude oil in the next decade. The outlook for the price of crude oil is uncertain. The annual rate of increase could be less than the 18 percent in nominal prices discussed in this chapter, but it could easily be more. The probability is great that it will be substantially greater than the 3 percent in real prices that is commonly used in projections for the next decade. That implies that the world, and particularly the oil-importing developing countries, will have extremely unpleasant problems in the next decade. The unpleasant nature of these problems is not a reason to avoid addressing them now.

17 Proposals for Solving the LDCs' Financial Problems

Francis Blee

Despite the optimism of the author, it is quite possible to envision a pessimistic scenario for the world over the next ten years, because clearly, as many of the other contributors to this book have pointed out the international monetary and economic system is under severe strain. A sudden or unexpected shock could conceivably collapse the system.

It is not necessary to describe the nature of such shocks, but, for example, the default of a key important country, a drastic interruption of oil flow from the Middle East, or a sudden major price increase in oil in real terms could collapse the system and bring back memories of the 1930s. Negative growth, high unemployment, rising protectionism, and a general reduction in living standards are consequences no one wants to experience. It must be admitted, however, that the probability of such an occurrence has certainly gone up over the last few years. However, this negative scenario can be avoided, but we need basic changes in the international monetary and economic system.

In a broader conceptual context, first of all, a closer tie between the international monetary system and real economic factors is needed. Second, there is a need for an expanded and more robust international monetary system. Third, there is need for greater boldness and ingenuity in facilitating international investment because clearly the risk has gone up substantially and the perceived return on investment has declined—if for no other reason than that of lower growth and higher energy prices. These concepts raise key issues that still must be answered. They underscore the theme of this book, critical challenges to the international monetary system.

We must address the interaction between the political, economic, and social forces and the international financial system. Specific measures that warrant further discussion follow: First, OPEC clearly must become a full partner in future international monetary discussions and negotiations. Second, we must have a strong linkage between the price of oil and the price of capital.

Next, I think we must secure the long-term investments of OPEC and other investor countries in the form of guarantees against the threat of political or economic expropriation. A country guarantee could perhaps be supported and backed up by some type of international guarantee, perhaps through the IMF. This can be likened to the Federal Reserve guarantee of bank deposits in the United States. Many times the existence of such a guarantee obviates the need for such a guarantee.

Clearly, to do this function a larger and expanded IMF will be needed to meet this challenge. In return guarantees must be obtained for a secure supply of oil—OPEC guarantees—so that if a shortfall occurs such as the current situation with Iran and Iraq standby capacity is in place and there will be a guarantee that the shortfall will be made up.

Finally, direct private investment by OPEC and the major investor countries in the LDCs is needed. This makes sound economic sense because clearly the highest return in the long term may well be available in the resource-rich LDCs, particularly Latin America and Africa. These are also the areas where the capital needs are the greatest. It is also clear that these countries have tremendous political and social tensions, which have been discussed, and therefore they must have capital investment and expanded income.

I am greatly concerned about debt, and I think these long-term investments have to take on more the nature of almost an equity investment. This type of direct investment will provide or offer the hope of a better return to the OPEC and other investor nations. The further challenge is to reduce the risk through the guarantees. With a higher risk-adjusted rate of return the inducement to invest should be much stronger.

The quid pro quo for this is the guarantee of the steady flow of oil by OPEC, and indeed I would also suggest that other oil exporters could be brought into this negotiation, including the non-OPEC countries such as Mexico or the North Sea countries.

Reasserting my basic optimistic nature, I would say in conclusion that all of the measures I have described can be accomplished. We only need to reach out and seize the opportunity.

18 International Capital Markets and the Semi-Industrialized Nations

Carlos Diaz Alejandro

The first duty of an international capital market is to move capital from capital-rich to capital-poor countries. This naturally involves current-account deficits on the part of capital-importing countries and debt accumulation, at least for long periods of time.

The world has witnessed many regimes that transferred capital. The most successful, in relative magnitude, occurred under the Pax Britannica, with large transfers of funds to capital-poor countries, including the United States we have also seen the regime of 1945 to 1973 and the later troubles coming from adjusting the international financial system to post-1973 events. This is the challenge now; since 1973, we have entered a new transition. What this transition leads to is uncertain.

It should also be stated that most of the developing countries of today had no role in shaping the institutions and the rules of the game of the postwar Bretton Woods system. In 1944 most of the LDCs were colonies. Only the Latin American countries, India, and a few other LDCs were present at Bretton Woods, and India had not yet gained independence. So it should not be difficult to understand why the Bretton Woods regime was never seen by most LDCs as something of their own.

Even as late as the 1960s it was debated whether the SDRs should be extended outside the Group of Ten. For a while there were many people who said that SDRs should be kept within the Group of Ten, but fortunately the inflationary view prevailed.

It should be said that during this transition period (1973-1980) the international capital market has provided the less-developed countries with some pluses as well as some minuses. Here, of course, it is imperative to enter into the typology that has already been suggested for developing countries. One has at the very least to differentiate between OPEC, the newly industrialized countries—which have been the most active participants in this market—and the fourth world, encompassing the poorest of the developing countries.

As far as the international capital market is concerned, it has been the semi-industrialized countries—Brazil, South Korea, the Philippines—which benefited the most from international banking and Eurocurrency credits. They benefited in a number of ways: low real-interest rates and a gentler pace of adjustment to what came after 1973. This contrasts with aid, or even with insured suppliers' credits, untied as to countries and untied as to commodities. That was a great improvement.

The loans were at commercial rates but they were not a bad deal. The real-interest rate can be computed in different ways, but most would show that the real-interest rates that these countries paid for the credit, including spreads, were quite low, perhaps even negative under some calculations.

Last, but not least, of the benefits is the emergence of a fairly competitive international capital market giving the semi-industrialized countries flexibility in dealing with transnational corporations and the IMF. It allowed some depackaging of the Transnationals' bundle, long sought by developing countries. These countries also gained flexibility in dealing with the IMF, an institution that is not terribly popular in some developing countries. Import LDCs, such as Brazil and Colombia, have managed throughout this period to politely but firmly ignore the International Monetary Fund. This is the result not of Latin perversity, but of past disagreements when the IMF staff acted obtrusely and dogmatically. It is interesting to note that both Brazil and Colombia have registered some the highest sustained growth rates in Latin America.

It is a matter of record that profits of international banks dealing with LDCs have grown quite fast. Defaults, I understand, have been fewer in dealings with third-world countries than in domestic loans during the last few years. It is not obvious that lending to New York City and Chrysler is safer than lending to Turkey and Peru.

Part of the 1973-1980 story is that the fourth world was left out, but international capital markets could not have expected to handle it, given the rules of the game. Blame should be placed on the failure of the Organization for Economic Cooperation and Development (OECD) countries to meet aid targets, with the exception, one should remember, of the Dutch, the Scandinavians, and OPEC. We are told that aid targets were not met in the 1970s because of economic difficulties; but they were not met in the 1960s either.

The counterpart to the benefits obtained by the semi-industrialized countries in world capital markets fell on OPEC. They got fairly bad yields—the real returns from their financial investments were not great. One is not terribly heartbroken at that result for 1973-1980.

But this is economic history and we must ask: What about the 1980s? Will this situation continue? We have heard several forecasts. Their common denominator is tremendous uncertainty. "Slight" changes in a key variable like the real price of oil produce very different scenarios. If one changes OECD growth rates, one can get very different scenarios for nonoil LDCs. Will China become a very large borrower or not?

There are of course important political uncertainties, especially in the Middle East, where the legitimate national aspirations of the Palestinians must be reconciled with the equally legitimate security aspirations of the state of Israel. There are also forecasts saying that after the Iran-Iraq war both nations will have to rearm, reinvest, and produce a lot of oil, and that this may undo OPEC. The future is quite open and we cannot tell the exact configurations of what will happen.

But it is reasonably clear that the fourth world will be very dependent on aid, direct or indirect, although one can imagine that some countries on the border line between the semi-industrialized and the fourth world, like India, could very well begin to borrow massively on commercial terms. Many of these countries have slight debt positions.

The cartel scenario is one that is particularly gloomy for the semi-industrialized countries. Remember the discussions on the new international economic order in the last few years? Generally speaking, the LDCs said, "let us reform the international markets because they do not work." The industrialized countries replied, "markets are wonderful and they work quite efficiently; intervening in the commodity and other markets would be terrible; laissez faire!"

Now one is beginning to hear arguments, even from private bankers, that there is something wrong in the international financial market, that it cannot go on like this, that it is not working right. "We need bureaucrats to come and regulate it," they say. The bureaucrats, of course, are some of my best friends at the International Monetary Fund.

It is strange that private businessmen would want somebody else to come and get part of their business and to have bureaucrats regulating this market. A possible scenario would have the IMF supervising an "orderly market agreement" in the international credit market to keep competition from getting out of hand while providing certain information to the banks. Borrowers, especially the semi-industrialized countries, would face a common front of lenders. Another party that could be interested in this cartel is OPEC, which would receive financial assets with better yields than those obtained from 1973 to 1980. In exchange, OPEC would presumably provide a steady supply of oil to the OECD countries. So there is here a possible coalition including OPEC, industrialized countries, and the IMF. A country like Brazil or South Korea has reason to worry about this possibility. One would hope that there is not too much competition among banks of different nationalities to have that kind of situation come to pass.

Let us consider another possibility, the Chicken-Little scenario, involving massive LDC defaults. The LDC servicing record so far has been quite good. There have been some reschedulings but no recent repudiations that I am familiar with. In fact, econometric studies trying to predict defaults by LDCs face the problem that there have been so few defaults in recent years.

They have to go back to the 1930s, when almost the whole world was in default. Here one finds a lesson. One could argue that the defaults of the 1930s did not arise from bad loans to LDCs or from a perfidious unwillingness to pay. They arose from macroeconomic mismanagement in the industrialized countries and from their protectionism. The greatest chance of LDC defaults in the 1980s would arise if industrialized countries follow very recessive policies, or if they follow very protectionist policies.

Under those conditions defaults are not just likely to happen; in fact, LDCs would be foolish to attempt maintaining normal servicing of their debt. It would be foolish from their narrow viewpoint as well as from the viewpoint of the macroeconomic health of the international economy.

Neither the cartel nor the Chicken Little scenario are very probable events. Both, however, suggest that there will be a trend toward greater regulation of international capital markets. One could argue that substantial asymmetics exist today between national and international financial markets. In the national markets there are the banks. Where is the international lender of last resort? We have something like it, but not exactly like it. There is scope for clearer international lender-of-last-resort rules involving both the IMF and national central banks.

Before semi-industrialized LDCs accept this with enthusiasm, solid evidence would be needed that there is a new IMF, which has changed some of its past practices. There are some pieces of evidence pointing in their direction. In 1980 the IMF signaled changes in its lending policies, lengthening maturities and liberalizing conditionality. One is delighted and somewhat amused to hear the IMF adopt concepts like structural change. Participants in the intellectual debates between Latin American structuralists and the International Monetary Fund in the 1950s would chuckle. Nowadays when one talks about supply policy in the United States, this is associated with the New Right. Yet that was an old Latin American structuralist slogan; these structuralists would tell the IMF: "Demand management is not enough." People and institutions learn and it is a good thing to see that the IMF has learned.

That IMF transformation is not complete, but if the trend continues, if there are assurances that credit cartel arrangements will be avoided, and if distance between the IMF and the private banks is maintained so as to preserve competition in the international financial markets, then innovations to make the international financial system more robust would be met with interest by semi-industrialized countries. The flow of resources could be increased while making the system less vulnerable to catastrophic shocks.

One last point. It goes back to the Chicken Little scenario. What if things go very wrong, like in the 1930s? The semi-industrialized countries, one would think, would continue to grow, not unlike some of them grew in the 1930s. It is a stunning fact that Brazilian industrialization in the 1930s was faster than it was in the previous decade. Although the semi-industrialized have a stake in the international system the worst that could happen to them is not that terribly bad—the possibility of their default is not to be taken very seriously unless there is a massive international economic catastrophe. But that does leave out the fourth world, for which the need for aid remains very pressing.

Discussion

Question: It seems important that we at least put on our agenda that second major commodity system that is really no less important in human terms than the oil and energy system—a commodity system over which the United States has about as much control as Saudi Arabia has over oil and, of course, that is the world grain economy. There are strong linkages between energy prices and food prices. Food-grain prices are strongly conditioned by the cost of the inputs producing them and those, at least in many countries, are very energy intensive, fuel and nitrogen fertilizer being the leading ones. In addition, we are now beginning to ask our agricultural systems to provide energy as well, by way of the conversion of corn to alcohol. If this becomes a significant factor in the United States, it could make the exports of U.S. corn dwindle and make importing grain quite expensive.

How can the United States, the IMF, and the World Bank act in such a way as to encourage the developing countries to use the market signals associated with oil and food prices, to get their macro prices right, while at the same time recognizing that we cannot ask any government to use market signals to allocate resources if that allocation results in widespread hunger and starvation?

Answer: This is a very tangential answer, but there are many cases where attempts to keep food prices down have limited food production very severely. In fact, the protection of the city populations or the feeding of the city populations has been done at the expense of the farming populations and the balance of payments of the United States as a whole. Among the supply factors that are of interest to the Fund and the World Bank are the correct pricing of foodstuffs.

Answer: I would also like to interject one other factor, and that is population growth. The differential around the world, with zero to declining populations in the industrialized countries and the growth in population over the next twenty years heavily skewed toward the fourth world or the LDCs, underscores the need for direct foreign investments in agricultural facilities.

Question: I would like to share the pessimism of many of the contributors, but I find it difficult to understand fully the classification that is being used and particularly the method of classification developing countries.

I recall in 1970 being very much concerned about all the developing countries. By 1975, after the first oil price increase, I was not so much concerned about Algeria. I have forgotten about Mexico, and I have forgotten about Indonesia, not to mention Egypt. Looking at the situation now, there are again quite a number of developing countries that seem to be benefiting considerably from the increase in the price of oil. My concern, therefore, is whether we are not getting more and more concerned about less and less, and whether it would not be preferable to get some sort of better definition of the various countries. My question, put another way, is would it not be more useful to discuss the development needs of a group of countries and the financial need of some specific developing countries?

Answer: I understand the problem of the questioner. There is no more unmanageable problem than the classification of countries. It is difficult enough to find the economic criteria by which countries should be classified—whether Mexico, for example, belongs with the oil-exporting countries or not, on purely economic criteria. Unfortunately, it is perhaps no secret that countries have particular pet peeves as to where they should go in these classifications, and the international organizations are not entirely free to overlook these desires on the part of these countries.

Perhaps the greatest misclassification of all is the concept of developing countries, which now includes all but about twenty countries in the world. The per capita incomes of the developing countries range from those higher than Switzerland and Germany to the entire low end of the range, with degrees of industrialization that go far in all directions. Also, with some of them, there are general economic structures that are only a very little different from those of certain European countries that are classified as industrial.

I am deeply aware of the problem you refer to. Believe me, it is insoluble.

Question: Several of the contributors have suggested that there are possibilities of making arrangements between the industrialized countries and OPEC, with a link between energy and changes in the international monetary system. I am wondering where the grounds for optimism come from. We have been engaged in the United Nations for a year now trying to launch something called global negotiations. The idea was to negotiate with OPEC for some kind of trade-off between predictability in the supply and price of energy and changes in the international monetary system.

In a special session of the General Assembly in August and September the effort to launch these negotiations broke down. The treasuries of the developed countries are not interested in these changes, or at least they are not prepared to make the sort of commitments that would be attractive to OPEC or to the least-developed countries. Also, the major players in OPEC, certainly the Saudis, have shown not the slightest interest in this exercise in New York. What are the grounds for optimism that there can be some kind of link made between energy prices on the one hand and changes in the international monetary and financial system on the other?

Answer: That discussion must be moved to the economic summit meetings; it has to become a key item on the agenda in the summit meetings starting with the major countries and bringing the OPEC people into those negotiations, and then spreading that to the LDCs. One of the grounds for optimism is that the outlook is so pessimistic that it is clear we have to have change. Take the scenario that Dr. Karchere described (see chapter 16). I am not sure the system can stand an annual increase in oil prices of 18 percent and I am not alone in this view. So, perhaps, the ground for optimism is that the alternative is so pessimistic.

About the Contributors

Francis Blee is chief economist for Smith-Kline Corporation.

Angelo Calmon De Sa is president of Banco Economico of Brazil. He is the former Minister of Industry and Commerce of Brazil.

Carlos Diaz Alejandro is professor in the Department of Economics at Yale University. He received the Ph.D. in economics at the Massachusetts Institute of Technology. Dr. Diaz Alejandro is a member of the Academic Panel of the Group of Thirty.

William B. Eagleson, Jr., is chairman of the Board of Directors of The Girard Bank. He is director of a number of companies, including the Private Investment Company for Asia. Mr. Eagleson is a graduate of Lehigh University and The Wharton School of the University of Pennsylvania.

Roberto Guarnieri is director of the Venezuelan Investment Fund.

William Hood is director of research and economic counselor at the International Monetary Fund. Formerly, he was the Deputy Minister of Finance of Canada and professor of economics at the University of Toronto.

Alvin J. Karchere is the director of economics at IBM Corporation. He has served as a consultant to several U.S. government agencies. Dr. Karchere received the Ph.D. from the University of London.

Peter B. Kenen is director of the International Finance Section and professor of economics at Princeton University. He is a member of the Advisory Committee on Reform of the International Monetary System of the U.S. Treasury Department and has served as consultant to such groups as the Board of Governors of the Federal Reserve System and the U.N. Conference on Trade and Development. He is a member of the Group of Thirty.

David Lomax is group economic advisor to the National Westminster Bank. He received the Ph.D. in economics from Stanford University, and has worked at the Federal Reserve Bank of New York and the British Foreign Office.

Koei Narusawa is economic advisor to the president of the Bank of Tokyo. He joined the bank in 1948 and has been associated with several of their overseas offices including Düsseldorf, Hamburg, and London. He received the J.D. from the University of Tokyo.

Corrado Pirzio-Biroli is the economic counselor at the Washington Delegation of the European Communities to the United States. He received the Ph.D. in economics and business administration at the University of Rome, and two postgraduate diplomas at the Institute of Social Studies in The Hague. Prior to forming the European Communities he was advisor on economic planning to the Government of The Sudan.

Jacques Polak is executive director of the International Monetary Fund and a former advisor to the managing director of the Fund. He is a member of the Group of Thirty.

Kurt Richebacher is general manager of the Dresdner Bank. He was formerly director of research of Berliner Bank.

Robert Slighton is vice-president and director of International Economic Forecasting at Chase Manhattan Bank.

Robert Triffin is currently a senior advisor to the European Economic Community while teaching at the University of Louvain in Belgium and is also Professor Emeritus at Yale University. He has held prominent positions with the International Monetary Fund and European multilateral financial institutions. During his distinguished academic career, Professor Triffin has published widely on international finance and monetary affairs.

Cesar Virata is Prime Minister of the Philippines and, since 1970, has been the Minister of Finance. He was chairman of the Development Committee of the World Bank and International Monetary Fund, and chairman of the Board of Governors of the Asian Development Bank. He is a member of the Group of Thirty.

Henry Wallich is a member of the Board of Governors of the Federal Reserve System. Governor Wallich was a member of the President's Council of Economic Advisors from 1959 to 1961 and was Seymour Knox Professor of Economics at Yale University.

H. Johannes Witteveen is advisor to the Board of Managing Directors of Amsterdam-Rotterdam Bank and chairman of the Board of Directors of the Group of Thirty. From 1967 to 1971 he was First Deputy Prime Minister and Minister of Finance for the Netherlands.

About the Editor

Norman C. Miller is a professor in the Economics Department at the University of Pittsburgh. He received the Ph.D. in economics from the University of Pittsburgh, and has published widely on international finance and international capital flows. Professor Miller has also taught at Carnegie-Mellon University and spent 1972-1973 on leave as a full-time consultant to the U.S. Treasury Department.